time for beads

GPL GEORGESON PUBLISHING LIMITED

by Julie Jackson

Mill Hill beads used in this book were supplied by Tiffanies Treasures

Published by **Georgeson Publishing Limited**
P.O. Box 100-667
North Shore Mail Centre, Auckland,
New Zealand.
Email: GPL@georgeson.co.nz

ISBN No. 0-473-05794-8

Editor: Prue Georgeson
Photography: Maria Sainsbury
Layout and Illustrations: Andreena Buckton
                                 Noodle Design Corp.

Printed in New Zealand

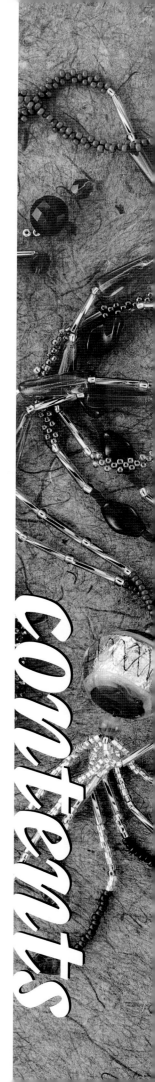

Colour Plates

introduction

I first became interested in beads about ten years ago on a trip overseas - I discovered the Bead Shop in Covent Garden. Some hours later, with a somewhat bruised and battered Visa Card I was away!

I have been lucky to have a daughter living in England and have therefore had several trips overseas, sometimes via Canada and the USA. Wherever I travel I seek out bead suppliers, antique or second hand shops, church fairs and local stalls looking for old necklaces. I have found Antique Fairs particularly useful in building up my selection of beads. Old family necklaces which are no longer wanted can be broken up and the beads from them used in many different ways.

Inspiration for my projects comes from many places including new and old books and magazines, these can be quite unrelated to beading but the design ideas are admired. I then 'mull over' colours, shapes and ideas before developing my own designs. I really enjoy making new projects and teaching them. Hand held bead work (as all these projects are) requires no special equipment, another advantage I feel.

Colours in beading are quite different from embroidery and this particularly appeals to me as they reflect against each other, changing with different combinations.

Beads are also extremely tactile. This is not something you are aware of until you start working with them and wearing them but you will find that they are very hard to leave alone!

Beads are another facet of embroidery. You are still working with a needle and thread but using beads not fabric, I hope you will find they are as enjoyable, pleasing and addictive to work with as I have and if you have as much enjoyment using this book as I have had writing it I will be very happy.

Julie Jackson, February 1999.

How to use this book

This book has been designed to introduce you to the fun of working with beads!

The projects are varied in their style and in the beads used to give you an insight into just some of the diverse range of projects that can be made using a needle, thread and bead.

This book is designed to lie flat on your lap for easy reference. Each project comes with all the instructions necessary for its completion. There is no need to flip between pages or sections, making this book an absolute delight to use. It has superbly clear illustrations and lots of them, with easy to follow instructions to make sure you find beading a most pleasurable activity.

———————

The first three projects are necklaces, the first is threaded, the next two introduce new techniques and beautiful beads to 'whet your appetite'.

The amulet purses are really enjoyable and satisfying little projects to make. They are made with seed and bugle beads which are widely available in a great selection of colours. It is quite possible to match your amulet purse to a special outfit.

If you are new to beading you may like to start with a purse that does not have a pattern - Midnight at the Beach - in this purse Mill Hill antique beads are used as these beads have most attractive tonal variations. There are different patterned purses to choose from so do try these also. Each purse features a different fringe and neckstrap treatment, a good way to learn some interesting variations. Making these purses is very satisfying and definitely addictive! When you feel a little more adventurous make 'Clematis' which is made using delica beads. Delica beads are slightly smaller allowing a more delicate pattern. Evening Star is made in peyote stitch. A technique used in the neckstraps of many of the different purses, full instructions are given for using this on a circular project.

The Rope Necklaces and Bracelet are great to make - we show them in a variety of colours so that you can see just how versatile this technique is. Gold and glitzy for evening or matching your favourite outfit for daytime!

If you want to try something a bit different see the Vessels or the Sculptured Bracelet and Necklace. These projects give you the opportunity to experiment more with the choice of beads used and the creation of your own pattern.

Each project is shown in full colour in the central pages of this book. They are shown full size so that the photos can serve as a very handy reference when you are stitching as well as an inspiration!

Embroiderers are generous people and frequently give away the hand made projects they have laboured over. Another joy of these beaded projects is that you can make them as a gift that will be most appreciated yet it won't have taken you too long.

With this book as your guide, enter with confidence into the world of beads!

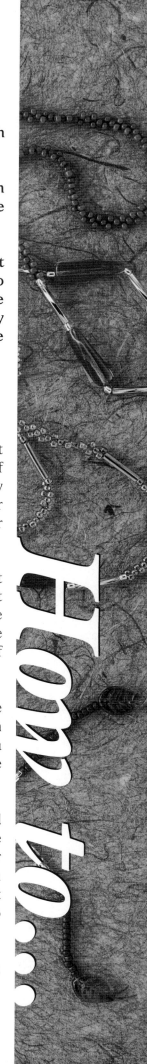

Beads have been used and admired throughout the ages and because they tend to be made from durable material very early examples of beads can be seen in museums around the world. Beads can be seen that were made hundreds of years before the Birth of Christ. The material beads were made from tended to reflect the development of the culture in which they were made and as technology developed so did the sophistication of the beads being made. With the development of bronze implements came the development of bronze beads and with the development of glass came glass beads. Historically they have been used in a variety of different ways by many different cultures, as items for barter, in religious ceremonies, on clothing and as jewellery and to denote status, wealth and power.

In more modern times the Victorian's used them, on bags, clothing and to enhance their embroidery. In the twenties they were used extensively on clothes and now in the nineties we are rediscovering the fun and fascination of beads.

Beads

Beads are a new and exciting medium to work with.

Choosing the colours of beads that you wish to work together is a little different from choosing threads to go together. Beads will change colour depending on the colour of the bead beside them. Interesting effects can be obtained by using 'flat' or 'opaque' beads (ie. without a shine like the 'antique' Mill Hill range of beads) besides 'shiny' or 'transparent' beads. When selecting beads for a project remember that patterns will not show up if you choose colours that are quite similar.

Bead sizing is determined by measuring across the outside diameter of the bead. The number given to the bead indicates the number of that bead that it takes to fill an inch. When a bead is described as size 11 this means that eleven of these beads will cover one inch. The larger the size number of a bead, the smaller the bead - a size 11 bead is smaller than a size 8. It is extremely difficult to make every bead the same size and variation in the size of beads is quite normal.

- Seed beads come in a variety of sizes, from very small to quite large. In this book I have mainly used size 11.
- Bugle beads can be twisted or plain and come in a variety of sizes from 7 mm to 30 mm. When using bugle beads check every single bead and discard any with sharp or rough edges as these will cut your thread.
- Delica beads are small cylindrical beads with a large hole, while they are called Size 11 they are actually nearer to a size 14.
- Delica drops are a small (4 mm) tear drop shape with a hole at one end.
- Donuts are round flat discs with large holes and come in a variety of sizes and colours.
- heishe beads are natural stone beads and have the appearance of a short fat bugle bead
- Crystal beads come in various sizes and tend to be round or oval. They are usually found in 'jewel' colours with cut facets.
- semi-precious stones are made from natural stone e.g. turquoise, lapiz, citrine and amethyst
- Square beads are as their name implies
- semi precious chips come in various sizes and are rough cut.

• hematites are steel grey square beads

The appearance of beads even of the same sort, e.g. seed beads varies tremendously.

Opaque beads cannot be seen through, nor can you see the thread inside the bead. An opaque bead will appear to come 'forward' when it is placed next to a transparent bead.
Transparent beads have a uniformly shiny finish and when used with matt beads, transparent beads come 'forward'.
Matt beads have a velvety or frosted surface and these recede visually in a design next to shiny beads.
Matt iridescent beads are both matt and iridescent, the colours have a 'shot' effect.
Metallic beads are glass beads with a shiny metallic surface coating which is usually baked on paint.

Throughout this book we give the quantity of beads required by weight or by the actual number required. As beads are sold in different sized packets check the weight required to work out the number of packet/s you will need to buy for each project.

Needles

Needles for beading need to be fine to fit through the hole in the bead not just once but several times depending on the pattern you are following. As with sewing needles the higher the number the finer the needle. Bead sizes and needle sizes do not correspond. Needles come in several lengths and generally the very fine ones are longer. The fine long needles are excellent to use when it comes to picking up long strings of beads for neckstraps or fringes but they will eventually develop a bend!

The shorter needles whilst not so fine are often easier to use, especially when you are 'stitching' the body of a bag or necklace etc.

Thread

Special thread is used for beading, this thread is stronger than ordinary thread and is waxed. The beading thread most commonly available is Nymo® thread. It is made of nylon and comes in a variety of colours. It comes in short lengths on a card in white and black and in bigger quantities on spools in a variety of colours. It is best to match the colour of the thread you use to the general colour of the beads being used. If you cannot match the thread to the beads I use a white thread and then colour it with felt tip pen to match the beads on the stitches which show!

Wax

It is extremely important to wax your thread before you start to use it as well as waxing it several times during the project. Wax your thread by pulling it through a block of beeswax. This is available from most beading and embroidery craft shops. The beeswax strengthens the thread, smooths down the fibres and helps it to slide through the beads.

Do not re-use thread which has been unpicked EVER!

Split rings

A split ring is a continuous double metal ring. Because the ring is double there is no gap for the thread to slip out, this makes it by far the most satisfactory choice for beading! Split rings are used as joining rings. They come in a variety of sizes and are used to attach a tassel to the body of the work.

Jump rings

A jump ring is a single metal circle and can be used to make a 'chain' by opening with pliers. The gap in a jump ring means the thread can slip out and this makes them most unsatisfactory to use in the projects in this book.

When using a joining ring use split rings

Keeper beads

A keeper bead is any bead tied on to prevent subsequent beads slipping off the end of the thread. It is tied on loosely so that it can be removed easily later (fig. 1).

Fig 1

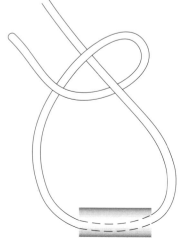

Turning bead

A turning bead is the bead on the end of a fringe. The thread is taken round the outside of the bead before going back through the bead next to it and returning the needle back up the fringe (fig. 2).

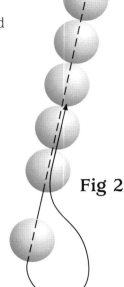

Fig 2

Small Pliers

These are extremely useful for breaking a bead that is in the wrong place without requiring you to undo the work.

Starting and Finishing Threads

Detailed notes on how to start each project are given with the project. To finish your thread at the end of a project take the thread back through half a dozen beads, work a clove hitch or little knot, repeat this two more times, then take the thread back through a few more beads before snipping the thread end off.

Starting and Finishing threads in the middle of Peyote stitch

Bring in a new thread when the old thread is about 20 cm in length. (This leaves sufficient thread to finish properly.) To start the new thread (leave a tail of 20 cm), wax then work the new thread through a few beads so that the thread comes out in exactly the same position as the old thread. Now carry on working with the new thread. You will find this method enables you to keep the pattern correct when you change threads.

When you have worked a further 10 - 12 beads finish off both thread ends. Pull both threads firmly to ensure that the bead work is firm, before taking first the old thread and then the new thread down through half a dozen beads and finishing in the manner described above. Try to avoid going through the same beads if possible when finishing off the thread ends.

Starting and finishing threads in the middle of Circular Brick Stitch (amulet purses and vessels)

Change thread when you have only 20 - 30 cms of thread left. Pick up a bead, take the thread down into the worked area of your purse and finish the thread in the usual manner. Take a new length of thread, wax and bring the new thread up through different beads in the amulet purse or vessel working catch stitches in the usual way, up to the position where the old thread came down through the last worked bead. Take the new thread up through the bead and continue stitching with the new thread (fig. 3).

When you are bringing in a new thread you work the first half of the stitch with the old thread and the second half with the new thread.

Fig 3

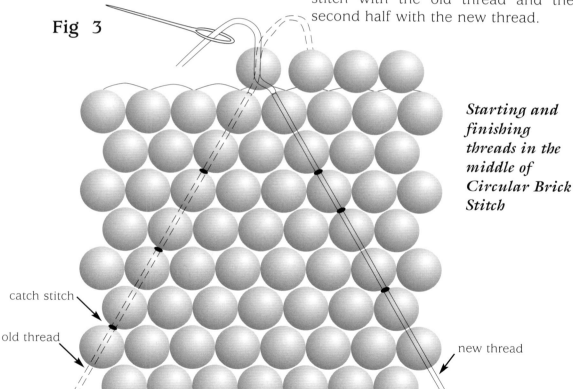

catch stitch

old thread

new thread

Starting and finishing threads in the middle of Circular Brick Stitch

Reading Patterns

When reading a beading pattern, the beads are indicated as individual motifs, ie. each oval represents one bead. The starting point for each pattern is indicated by an arrow - this is found at the bottom of each chart. When working with beads you work up a chart. The instructions given are the way I find it best to work. However any technique is acceptable if you are comfortable with it and achieve a good result!

– Lariat –

*T*he Lariat is a most useful necklace to dress up a shirt or jersey. It is simple to make and fun. I made this necklace out of two necklaces that I inherited. As they were I never seemed to use them but made up like this they have gained a 'new life' and seem to be just the right decorative touch for many occasions. If you have never worked with beads this necklace is a good place to begin! I have itemised the beads I used as a guide but either rummage round amongst your old bead necklaces for a couple with beads you fancy or go to your bead shop and buy a selection of beads that appeal to you!

Materials

I have given a comprehensive list of the beads used - do not worry about getting these exact beads, rather use them as a guide so that you can see just what an assortment of beads can be used together to create a pleasing new necklace.

- Selection of toning size 11 beads, iridescent, crystal (silver lined) and matt plum colour 4 grams of each

- 2 grams size 8 hematite beads (these are steel grey squarish beads in appearance)

- 2 grams 3 mm silver tubes

- 12 x 6 mm amethyst crystals

- 1 x 1 cm antique amethyst

- 6 x 8 mm amethyst coloured crystal beads

- 4 x 6 mm clear crystals

- 10 x 8 mm diameter petal shaped beads

- 22 x 4 - 5 mm square (some variation in size) pale amethyst coloured glass beads

- 6 x 1 cm oblong amethyst coloured beads

- 4 x 1 cm flat oval pale amethyst coloured beads

- long beading needle

- Nymo® thread to match, if matching coloured thread is not available use black for darker coloured beads and white with light coloured beads.

- wax

- 2 x 5 mm split rings

Finished length 140 cm (excluding tassels) or alter to suit your taste.

Refer to the colour photograph on page 38

Technique

Threading

Instructions

Divide each style of bead in half so that each side of your lariat will match. Work out how the beads are going to be arranged on your lariat - remember you only have to work out half the pattern as the second half will be a mirror image of the first.

Creating A Pattern

I did little arrangements with the 'different' beads and then separated the 'arrangements' with 20 or 30 seed beads sometimes less.

I started with a 1 cm oblong amethyst bead then used five matt wine coloured seed beads followed by a silver square tube alternating with a square amethyst three times then 20 pearl iridescent coloured seed beads.

My next little arrangement was a hematite bead, square amethyst, hematite bead, 15 crystal seed beads then a square amethyst, a clear crystal then a square amethyst, followed by 15 more crystal seed beads. Continue

in this manner until you have arranged half the length required. Next select a feature bead - I used the 1 cm antique amethyst. (This goes at the centre of your lariat and when the necklace is doubled and worn it will be at the front of your neck).

With your arrangement sorted the beads are now ready to thread. Cut your thread four times the finished length plus 50 cm (6.1 m) and wax. Thread one of the split rings on to the thread and slide halfway along the thread. Now thread both thread ends through your needle, (fig 1).

Pick up the beads as arranged to the half way point, now add the feature bead. Reverse the order and thread the other half of the beads on - when you have a similar arrangement to the first half of the necklace slide on another split ring and then take your needle with the two threads in it back to the beginning. If you find you cannot take the needle back through all the beads with both threads in it, take the thread back to the beginning one thread at a time.

To finish off the two threads take one thread at a time round the first split ring then thread it back up the lariat finishing in the usual manner. Refer to page 8 for detailed instructions on finishing.

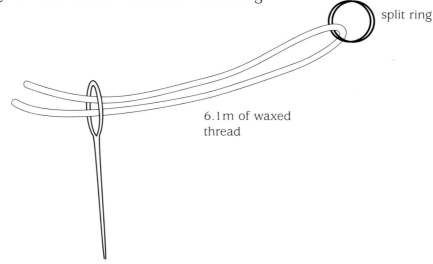

split ring

6.1 m of waxed thread

Fig 1

Tassel

The tassels provide a very nice finishing touch to your lariat. Each tassel is made up of three strands of different lengths with a different assortment of beads on each length. I used a combination of crystal and iridescent seed beads along with two 'different' beads on each tassel. One somewhere along the length of the tassel and one at the end.

Cut a 1 m length of thread, wax well. Tie on a seed bead as a keeper bead 20 cm from the end (remember to tie it on loosely!) for more information on keeper beads refer to page 8.

The first strand of the tassel is worked up from the keeper bead, the keeper bead will be the bottom 'turning' bead of the first tassel. Now add a feature bead then a variety of other beads including a second feature bead working towards the split ring. (My tassels vary from 4 - 6 cm in length). Take the thread around the ring twice before starting the next strand of the tassel, (fig. 2).

Pick up the beads for the second tassel in a pleasing arrangement including a feature bead along with the seed beads, when the tassel is the desired length add another feature bead then a seed bead as your 'turning bead' and take the thread back to the split ring, for more information on 'turning beads' refer to page 8.

Fig 2

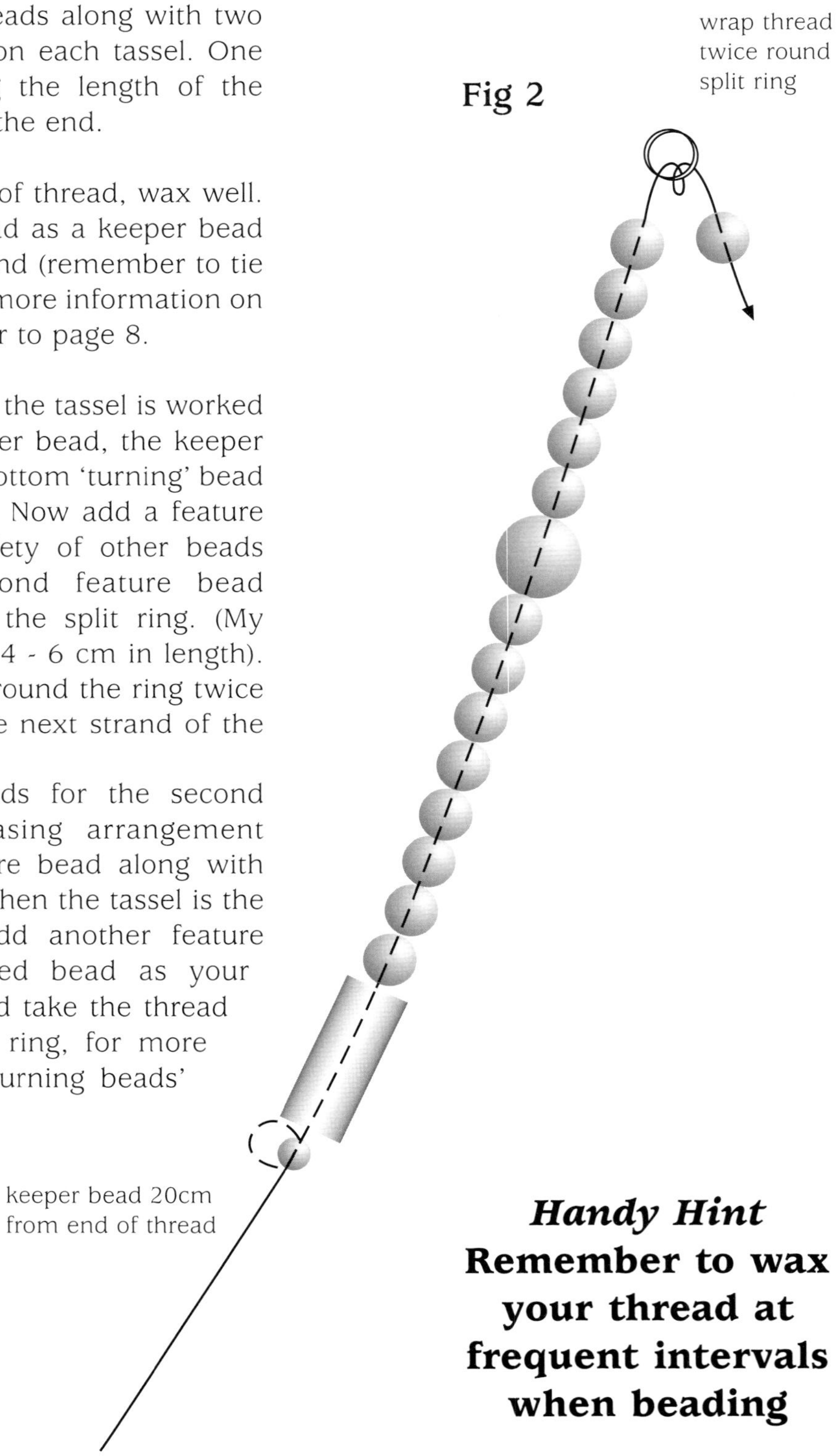

wrap thread twice round split ring

keeper bead 20cm from end of thread

***Handy Hint*
Remember to wax your thread at frequent intervals when beading**

Take the thread round the ring twice and you are ready to make the third strand of the tassel. This may be repeated as many times as desired to make as many strands to your tassel as you would like. Vary the length of each strand and change the arrangement of beads on each tassel (fig. 3).

When you have made the desired number of strands to your tassel take your needle and thread around the split ring twice then down through the last strand that you have just completed and finish in the usual manner.

To finish the first strand of the tassel undo the knot on the keeper bead and using this bead as your turning bead take the thread back towards the split ring, go round the ring twice before finishing the thread in the usual way.

Variation:

A larger bead may be used at the beginning just below the split ring and all the threads go through it before going around the ring.

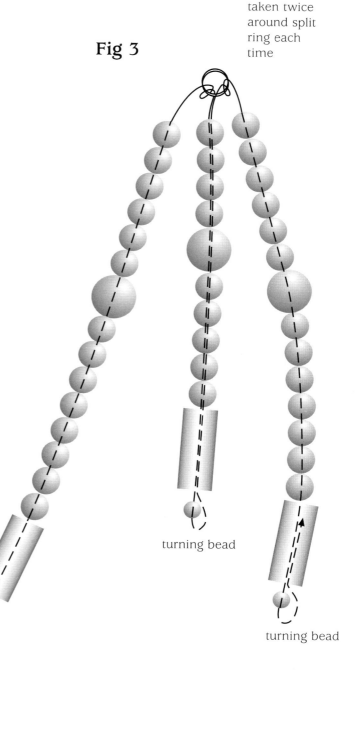

Fig 3

thread taken twice around split ring each time

turning bead

turning bead

keeper bead 20cm from end of thread

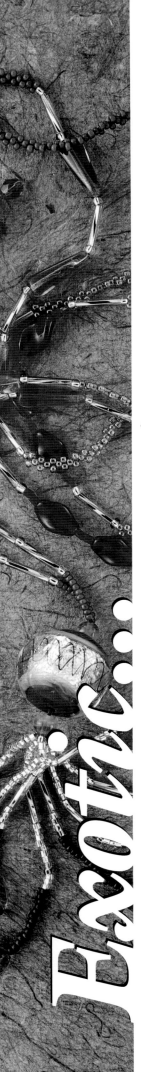

Exotic Bead Necklace

The inspiration for this necklace came with the purchase of one rather gorgeous exotic bead. I bought this special hand-blown glass bead at a craft market but look around at whatever is available near you and choose one special bead to be the centrepiece of your necklace. Once you have chosen the main bead choose a variety of other beads to go with it in different shapes and sizes to compliment the main bead and give additional visual interest.

Materials

- One large exotic bead

- 2 x 5 mm semi precious jade beads - these go either side of the exotic bead

- Selection of bugle beads, fancy beads and seed beads

- 5 grams size 11 olive green opaque seed beads

- 5 grams size 11 iridescent green seed beads

- 2 grams gold seed beads

- 1 gram royal blue seed beads

- 5 grams 12 mm long gold twisted bugles

- 1 gram 12mm long green bugle beads

- 10 x 15 mm long semi twist light blue

- 6 x 10 mm long flat twist royal blue beads

- 8 x 1 cm lime green leaves

- Nymo® thread to match

- wax

- beading needle long or short

Refer to the colour photograph on page 43

Technique

Threading, peyote stitch

Instructions

Divide the fancy beads in half so that each side of your necklace will match. Work out how the beads are going to be arranged - remember you only have to work out half the pattern as the second half will be a mirror image of the first. Start and finish with 10 seed beads, this keeps the end of the necklace nice and 'fluid'. (Detailed information on creating a pleasing pattern is given with the lariat on page 11.)

Cut and wax a length of thread twice the desired length plus 80 cm. This necklace is 1.2 m long so the thread required is 3.2 m if you make your necklace the same as mine.

Fold the thread in half and thread the doubled thread through the needle.
Tie a keeper bead 40 cm from the end of your threads, (fig. 1). This keeper bead will be removed and the exotic bead will be threaded on here when your necklace is nearing completion so tie it with a knot that can be undone!

Pick up 10 seed beads to start forming the neckstrap, now pick up half your beads in the order that you have decided on to form a pleasing pattern. At the half way point start reversing your arrangement of beads until you are back to the final 10 seed beads which match the beginning. Tie on the last seed bead as a keeper bead, once again with a knot that can be undone! This is to prevent the beads falling off your thread while you take a second doubled thread through the neckstrap.

Cut a second length of thread as above, wax, fold in half and use double as before. Take the doubled thread through the full length of the necklace. This will give four threads going through each bead. If you find you can't take the doubled thread through the beads in one movement, take one thread through at a time. If you can't take four threads through, three will be adequate.

Fig 1

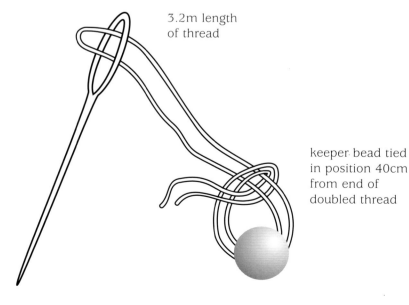

3.2m length
of thread

keeper bead tied
in position 40cm
from end of
doubled thread

– Exotic bead necklace –

To give added interest to the neck strap in the areas where you have used seed beads (except for the first and last 10 seed beads) pick the seed beads up in peyote stitch. To work peyote stitch pick up a bead, miss a bead and take the needle through the next bead, (fig. 2). It is very simple but will give added eye appeal to the neck strap. Do not pull the thread too tight and if need be manoeuvre the beads into position with your finger nail! (See fig. 3)

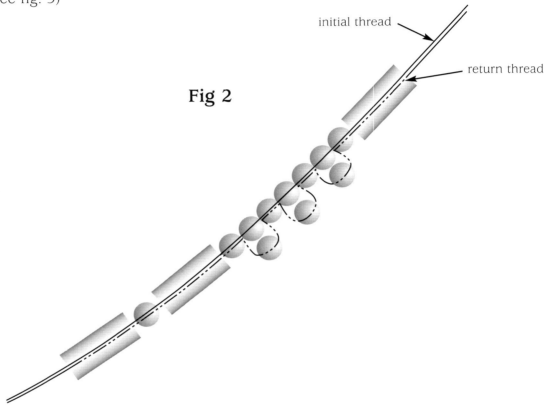

Fig 2

initial thread

return thread

Fig 3

final position of beads in peyote stitch

With the second length of thread taken through the full length of the necklace - you now have four lengths of thread going through the beads. Remove keeper beads and take the eight thread ends, one or two threads at a time, through a 5 mm bead, the exotic bead and then through another 5 mm bead ready to form the tassel.

The tassel

Each of the eight thread ends, is used to form a tassel. The tassels are made with gold seed and bugle beads, olive green seed beads with a feature 'leaf' bead at the end of each tassel. Make each tassel different, different in length, number of various beads used etc. Fiddle until you have created a pleasing arrangement - and have fun!

I picked up different numbers of gold seed beads placing a gold bugle bead sometimes in the middle of the gold seed beads and sometimes at the end of the seed beads. Some tassels have olive green seed beads after the gold beads and just before the leaf bead others do not have any green beads - all tassels finish with a leaf bead (fig. 4).

To finish the tassels, turn on the leaf bead and take the thread back up the tassel. The first four threads finished should go back to the main part of the necklace to be finished in the usual way. (Work a catch stitch and then weave the thread through half a dozen or more beads, repeat this three times). The other four threads are finished by taking the thread back to the top of the tassel then down through a neighbouring tassel and working the usual catch stitches to complete.

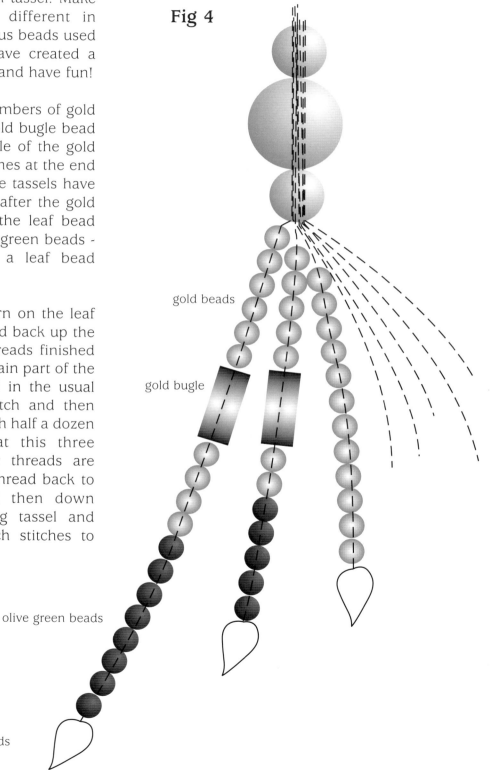

Fig 4

gold beads

gold bugle

olive green beads

leaf beads

Turquoise Necklace

This necklace is a most useful fashion accessory. The asymmetric design adds visual interest and it is fun to try using some of the different beads that are available. The donuts and chips are easy to use and combined with the heishe and seed beads give the necklace the added interest of different shapes, tones and finishes. There are many different colours available so make your necklace to suit your wardrobe or give it as a gift for someone special.

Materials

- 1 x 3 cm donut

- 2 x 1.5 cm donuts

- 2 grams turquoise delica beads

- 5 grams turquoise chips

- 2 grams silver seed beads

- 1 strand turquoise heishe beads

- 25 silver tubes

- Nymo® thread to match beads

- wax

- two beading needles - long or short

- clasp

Refer to the colour photograph on page 40

Technique

Threading and peyote stitch

Instructions

This necklace is worked in two separate parts, the first side is completed before starting the second side.

To work the first side of the Necklace (little donut further from big central donut)
Cut a 1 metre length of thread and wax, tie a keeper bead 20 cm from one end of the thread. Pick up enough delica beads to go through the hole in

18

the large donut and form a 'snug' circle around the donut, position the delica beads about 10 cm from the keeper bead. The number required will depend on the size of your donut.

Then take the beads away from the donut, lie them out straight and take your needle back through the second to last bead and work peyote stitch back to the starting bead. To work peyote stitch pick up a bead, miss a bead and take the needle through the next bead, (fig. 1).

Fig 1

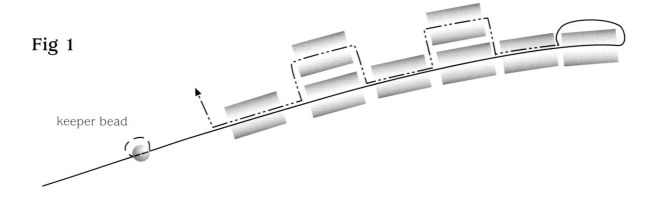

keeper bead

Fig 2

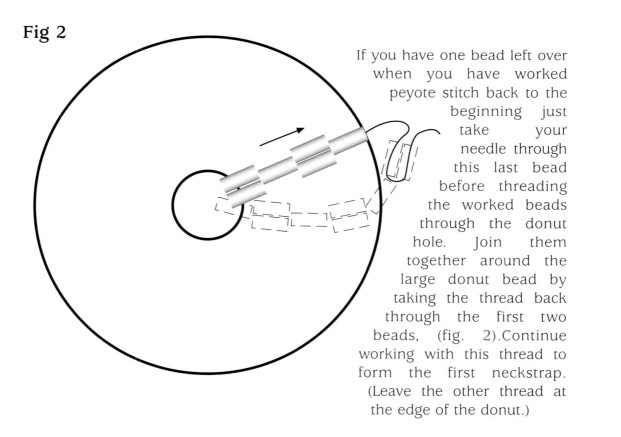

If you have one bead left over when you have worked peyote stitch back to the beginning just take your needle through this last bead before threading the worked beads through the donut hole. Join them together around the large donut bead by taking the thread back through the first two beads, (fig. 2).Continue working with this thread to form the first neckstrap. (Leave the other thread at the edge of the donut.)

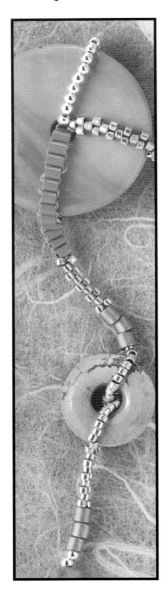

Pick up six delica beads then a selection of the other beads in any order for 5 cm.

Now pick up turquoise delica beads for 4 cm and go through the hole in one of the small donuts. The delica beads are nice and manoeuvrable around the donut. (The donut bead is not anchored at this point and will slide up and down but this does not matter.)

Continue to pick up a selection of beads for 6 cms. Now change to heishe beads for the final 10 cm . Adjust the length of the necklace at this point, if desired. Attach one end of the clasp firmly by stitching around it three times and then return your needle through the beads down to the little donut.

When you are using delica beads in the main part of the necklace always work them in Peyote stitch.

When you reach the delica beads leading up to the donut work peyote stitch for about 1 cm down to the donut, pick up 16 delica beads (or thereabouts) - do not work peyote stitch with these beads - and go through the small donut the opposite way. This secures the donut in the correct position on your necklace. Work the delica beads on the other side of the donut in peyote stitch.

Continue taking the thread back to the central donut (remembering to work peyote stitch when you come across delica beads) When you have taken your thread right back to the big central donut finish your thread off securely in the usual manner. (For detailed information on finishing threads refer to page 8.) Finish the other thread end in the same way.

Fig 3

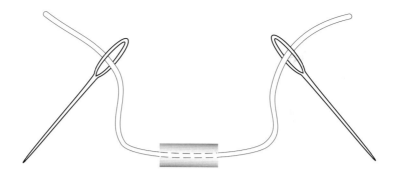

To work the Second Side of the Necklace

Cut a 1 m length of thread, wax and thread both ends with a beading needle then pick up one heishe bead positioning it in the middle of your thread, (fig. 3). Pick up a second heishe bead and thread a needle through it from each end, (fig. 4). Position the second bead on top of the first bead. Continue in this manner (fig. 5) until you have sufficient heishe beads joined together to wrap round the donut bead, join the length together by taking both needles back through the first heishe bead.

Fig 4

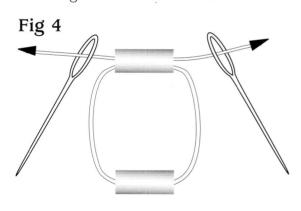

Fig 5

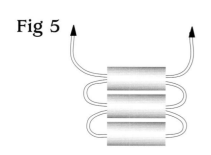

Add three more heishe beads, now drop one thread and continue to work with one thread only. Pick up a selection of your beads in any order for the next 2 cm. Pick up 3 cm of delica beads and go through the hole in the second small donut. (As on the first side at this point it is not anchored and will slip around.) Now pick up a selection of your beads in any order for 9 cm before picking up 10 cm of heishe beads. (If you adjusted the length on the other side adjust it here to match).

Attach clasp firmly before threading your needle back through all the beads down to the little donut. Remembering that when you have used delica beads in the neckstrap to work them in peyote stitch.

When you reach the little donut pick up 16 delica beads (or thereabouts) and go through the little donut in the opposite way. Continue to thread your needle back through your beading taking the thread to the centre of the large donut down through the heishe beads. At the centre pick up enough seed beads (I used silver ones) to fit around the donut in a firm loop, then finish off the thread end securely in the usual manner. Finish off the remaining thread end by the heishe beads also. Your necklace is complete, wear and enjoy it!

Midnight at the Beach

Midnight at the Beach has been made without a pattern in it but taking advantage of the interesting tonal variations found in Antique beads, you could use a selection of beads of a similar colour mixed together randomly and this would be equally satisfactory. I have used size 8 seed beads and matching square beads in the neckstrap along with the size 11 seed and bugle beads used in the purse. If you preferred, the neckstrap could be made just using the size 11 seed and bugle beads. Amulet purses are very satisfying to make and wear. This purse gives you the opportunity to concentrate on learning the technique without having to follow a pattern. It is a great place to start!

Materials

- 10 grams size 11 Antique Mill Hill steel grey/blue seed beads
- 4 grams 7 mm bugle beads
- 5 grams size 8 seed beads (neck strap)
- 2 grams square beads (neckstrap)
- Nymo® thread to match
- wax
- two short beading needles

Refer to the colour photograph on page 41

Technique

circular brick stitch

Instructions

First Row - bugle beads

Cut a 1.5 m length of thread, wax and thread both ends with a beading needle then pick up one bugle bead positioning it in the middle of your thread, (fig 1).

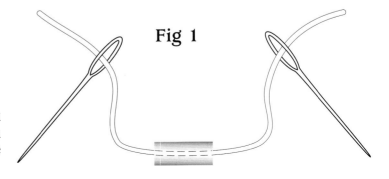

Fig 1

22

Fig 2

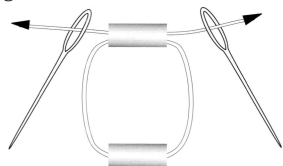

Fig 3

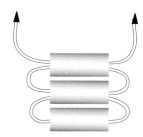

Pick up a second bugle bead and thread a needle through it from each end, (fig 2). Position the second bead on top of the first bead, then repeat with a third bead (fig. 3). It is important that the bugle beads are not pulled too tightly together when you are stitching them as the seed beads which are worked in the next row are a little bigger than the bugle beads and won't sit nicely if the bugle beads are stitched too tightly.

Continue in this manner until 42 bugle beads have been threaded. Join in a circle by taking both threads back through the first bead, continue threading through two or three more beads to form a firm circle and finish with one needle on each side of the beads (fig. 4 & 4a). Take off one needle.

Fig 4

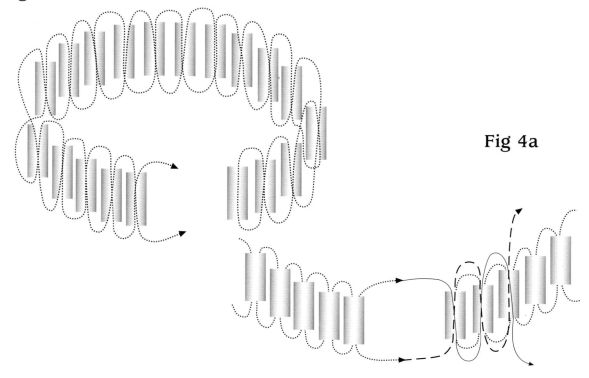

Fig 4a

Second row to finish - seed beads

Pick up two seed beads and stitching towards yourself, bring the needle under the thread between the second and third bugle bead (fig. 5). Now take the needle back up through the second bead (fig. 6).

Do not pull the first two beads too tight as the first bead must have sufficient thread to sit down flat when it is stitched in place at the end of the first row.

Fig 5

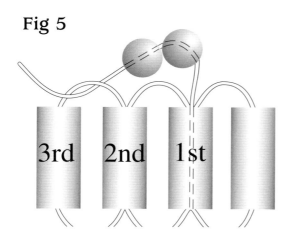

Fig 6

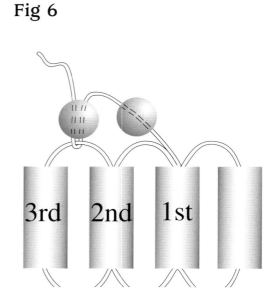

Now pick up *just one* seed bead and take the needle under the thread joining the third and fourth bugle beads together, return the needle back up through the centre of the seed bead, continue in this way working around the circle picking up one bead at a time, taking the thread under the thread between the bugle beads and back up the seed bead each time until the end of the row (fig. 7).

Fig 7

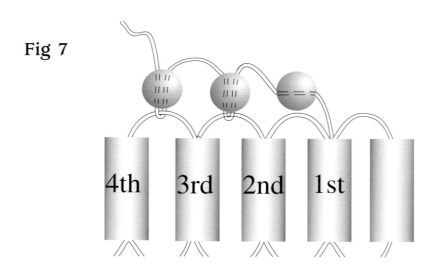

Fig 8

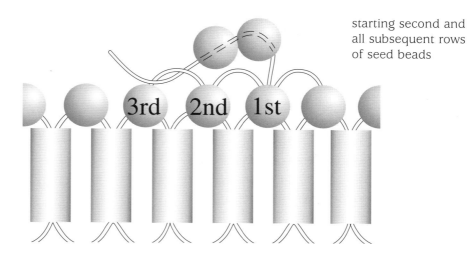

starting second and all subsequent rows of seed beads

At the end of the row go down through the first bead, take the needle under the thread between the bugle beads and come back up the first bead in the usual way.

The first row the needle is taken under the thread between the bugle beads, all following rows the needle is taken under the thread between the previous row of seed beads (fig. 8).

Work five rows stitching to the right and then reverse your stitching and work five rows to the left. Change in this way throughout the purse to prevent a bias forming

Continue working like this until you have worked 30 rows in total. If you run out of thread whilst stitching your purse refer to page 9 for detailed information on changing threads when working circular brick stitch.

When you have worked thirty rows, decide which is to be the front and back (position any unevenness - often found at the start of each row at the back of the purse) before oversewing the purse firmly together across the bottom. It is important to sew the purse firmly together at the base as

the fringe is attached to this oversewing. Finish off the thread in the body of the purse (for detailed information on finishing threads refer to page 8).

Go back to the top of the purse and using the thread left at the very beginning sew a row of seed beads on top of the bugle beads in the usual way to complete the purse. Finish the thread off securely. This can be done at any time during the construction of the purse.

Handy Hint
Count out 42 seed beads for each row and keep them separate to ensure that you stitch the right number of beads on each row of your purse.

Neck Strap

Cut a length of thread, twice the desired length plus 50 cm, wax. The thread is doubled to get the desired length but you actually work with a single thread. Attach the thread securely in the seed beads below the bugle beads in the main body of the purse. Then take the thread up through the bugle beads at one side of the top of the purse. Pick up six seed beads, then pick up a selection of beads until you reach the half way point. I have alternated seed, bugle and size 8 seed beads along with square beads.

Now reverse the arrangement of beads until you are back to the final six seed beads, which match the beginning. Take your thread down through the bugle beads and work through some of the seed beads, working the odd clove hitch to secure the neckstrap before going back up through the same bugle bead, then through the entire neckstrap and down into the purse before finishing the thread securely amongst the seed beads. On the return journey to create additional visual interest there are areas of double beads. To do this pick up three new beads go back through the main neckstrap for one bead, then pick up three more beads before going back into the main neckstrap again. I have done this four times at 3 - 4 cm intervals up the neckstrap (fig. 9).

Fig 9

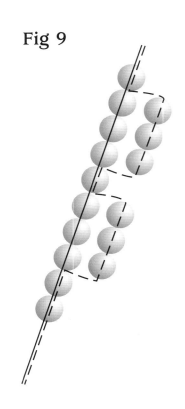

Handy Hint
keep the design simple at the centre of the neck strap as when worn this will be a the back of your neck

Fringe

The fringe on this amulet purse is rather lush! It is made up of two rows, with a shorter one at the front and a longer one at the back. It is simple to make using only the seed and bugle beads used in the purse.

To make a fringe cut a 1.5 m length of thread and wax. Secure the thread firmly in the 'body' of the purse bringing the needle out at the bottom left hand corner of the purse, catch the thread securely in the oversewing across the base of the purse.

Always start each strand of the fringe with two seed beads as this gives the fringe a nice fluid movement.

Front row of fringe

The first strand of the fringe has the two seed beads, (mentioned above) one bugle bead, two seed beads, a bugle bead and is turned with three seed beads. To turn with three seed beads pick up three seed beads at once and then take your needle up the bugle, the three beads position themselves very nicely at the base of the bugle (fig. 10).
Take the needle back up through all the beads on the strand of the fringe and anchor the thread with a catch stitch into the oversewing at the base of the purse ready to begin the second strand of the fringe.

The second strand of the fringe has the two seed beads, one bugle bead, three seed beads, one bugle bead and is turned with three seed beads. Continue like this adding an extra seed bead in the same position each time until you get to the centre when you work back to the other side reducing one seed bead from the same position in each strand. This creates a nice chevron finish to the fringe. Work your thread end back into the body of the purse and finish.

Back row of fringe

Take a second length of thread 1.5 m long, wax. Secure the thread firmly in the 'body' of the purse bringing the needle out at the bottom left hand corner of the purse, behind the front row of fringe, catch the thread securely in the oversewing across the base of the purse.

The first strand in the second row has two seed beads and a bugle bead, repeat 4 times then turn with three seed beads. To create a nice chevron shape to this side each strand is started with two seed beads and a bugle (x 3) but an additional seed bead is added each time before the last bugle bead up to the centre and taken off after the centre. On completion work the thread end back into the purse.

Your purse is now complete, enjoy wearing it and the compliments you will receive!

Fig 10

– Fractured Charm –

Fractured Charm is the second amulet purse made with circular brick stitch. It is a little smaller than 'Midnight on the Beach' and introduces a simple pattern. It is made using iridescent beads in shades of wine, teal, gold, royal blue, pink and green. Iridescent beads were chosen as they have an attractive shiny finish and the different colours blend well together. On the fringe and in the neck strap I couldn't resist using some 4 mm topaz and smoky blue coloured cut crystal beads and some 8 mm smoky blue cut crystal beads. Use of these different beads is optional and if you prefer you can make a most attractive fringe using the seed and bugle beads used in the purse. (Refer to the fringe on Midnight on the Beach page 27.) This purse is a dainty addition to your wardrobe and the pattern is a joy to follow!

Materials

- 10 grams size 11 iridescent green seed beads referred to as 'main' colour
- 2 grams seed beads of six different colours, wine, teal, gold, royal blue, pink, pale green
- 4 grams 7 mm iridescent green bugle beads
- 2 grams 15 mm iridescent green bugle beads (neckstrap)
- 14 x 8 mm smoky blue cut crystal beads (fringe and neckstrap)
- 30 x 4 mm smoky blue cut crystal beads (fringe and neckstrap)
- 30 x 4 mm topaz cut crystal beads (fringe and neckstrap)
- 8 x 4 mm royal blue cut crystal beads (neckstrap)
- Nymo® thread to match
- wax
- two short beading needles

refer to colour photograph page 41

Technique

circular brick stitch

Instructions

Foundation Row - bugle beads
Cut a 1.5 m length of thread, wax and thread both ends with a beading needle then pick up

one bugle bead positioning it in the middle of your thread (fig. 1). Pick up

Fig 1

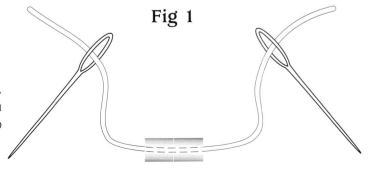

Fig 2

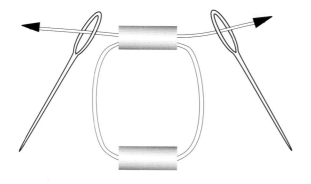

Fig 3

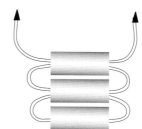

a second bugle bead and thread a needle through it from each end (fig 2). Position the second bead on top of the first bead, repeat with a third bugle (fig. 3). It is important that the bugle beads are not pulled too tightly together when you are stitching them as the seed beads which are worked in the next row are a little bigger than the bugle beads and won't sit nicely if the bugle beads are stitched too tightly.

Continue in this manner until 36 bugle beads have been threaded. Join in a circle by taking both threads back through the first bead, continue threading through two or three more beads to form a firm circle and finish with one needle on each side of the beads (fig. 4 & 4a). Take off one needle.

Fig 4

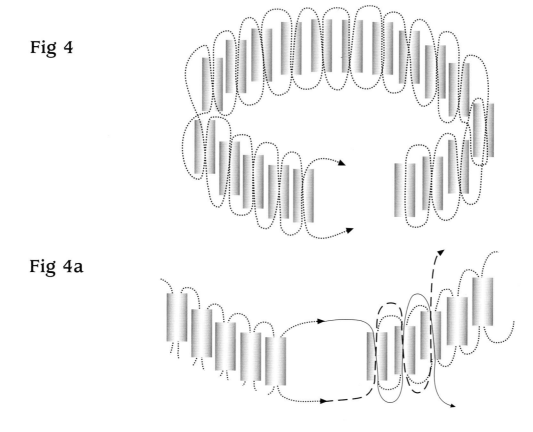

Fig 4a

Row 1 - seed beads

*Now using your main colour seed beads pick up two seed beads and stitching towards yourself, bring the needle under the thread between the second and third bugle bead (fig. 5).

Now take the needle back up through the second bead (fig. 6).

Do not pull the first two beads too tight as the first bead must have sufficient thread to sit down flat when it is stitched in place at the end of the first row.

Fig 5

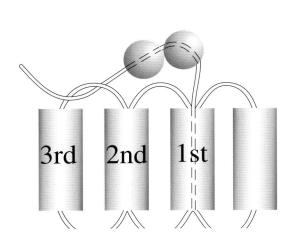

Fig 6

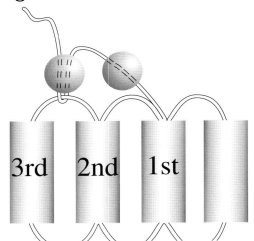

Now pick up *just one* seed bead and take the needle under the thread joining the third and fourth bugle beads together, return the needle back up through the centre of the seed bead, continue in this way working around the circle picking up one bead at a time, taking the needle under the thread between the bugle beads and back up the seed bead each time until the end of the row (fig. 7).

Fig 7

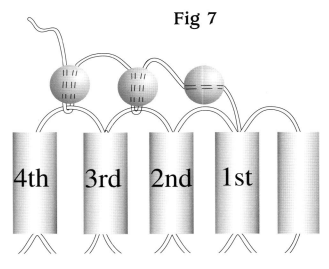

Fig 8

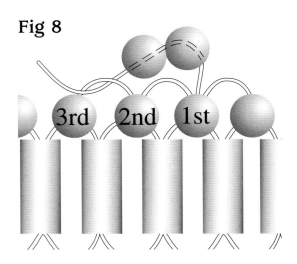

At the end of the row go down through the first bead, take the needle under the thread between the bugle beads and come back up the first bead in the usual way.*

Rows 1 - 3 are worked in the main colour only from * - *.(After Row 1 the needle will be taken under thread joining the seed beads in the previous row.) (Fig 8).

Handy Hint
Count out 36 seed beads for each row and keep them separate to ensure that you stitch the right number of beads on each row of your purse.

Following the Chart

When making an amulet purse in circular brick stitch you start at the top of the purse with the row of bugle beads and work up from these. For this reason you start at the bottom of the chart and work up. The arrow shows the starting point.

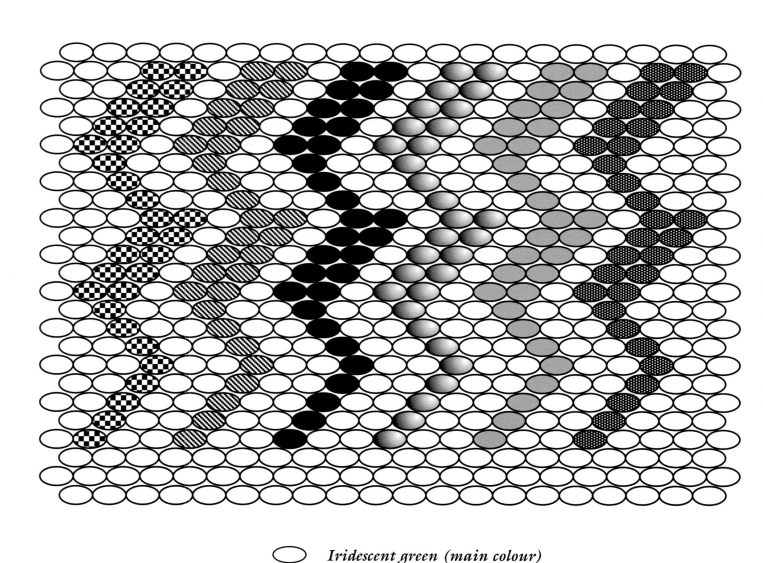

 KEY

Iridescent green (main colour)

Wine

Teal

Gold

Royal blue

Pink

Pale Green

Row 4 to Finish

The pattern starts in the fourth row and is worked on the front of the purse. To follow the chart and centre the design, work ten main beads then follow the chart by working one contrast bead, two main, one contrast, two main etc and follow on from there stitching in the usual way. As you are working put a line through the chart, or use felt tip pens to mark off the area you have worked.

Work five rows stitching to the right and then reverse your stitching and work five rows to the left. Change in this way throughout the purse to prevent a bias forming.

If you run out of thread whilst stitching your purse refer to page 9 for detailed information on changing threads when working circular brick stitch.

When you have worked the pattern position it on the front of your purse, (it will extend just slightly round the sides) before oversewing the purse firmly together across the bottom. It is important to sew the purse firmly together at the base as the fringe is attached to this oversewing. Finish off the thread in the body of the purse (for detailed information on finishing threads refer to page 8.)

Go back to the top of the purse and using the thread left at the very beginning sew a row of seed beads on top of the bugle beads in the usual way to complete the purse. Finish the thread off securely. This can be done at any time during the construction of the purse.

Neck Strap

Cut a length of thread, twice the desired length plus 50 cm, wax. The thread is doubled to get the desired length but you work with a single thread. Attach the thread securely in the seed beads below the bugle beads in the main body of the purse. Then take the thread up through the bugle beads to one side, at the top of the purse. Pick up five seed beads, then pick up a selection of beads until you reach the half way point. I have interspersed the feature beads (4mm royal blue and topaz crystal, 4 and 8 mm smoky blue crystal and 15 mm green iridescent bugles) with seed beads in a reasonably haphazard design, refer to the colour photograph page 41 for additional detail.

Now reverse your arrangement of beads until you are back to the final five seed beads, which match the beginning. Take your thread down through the bugle beads and work through some of the seed beads, working the odd clove hitch to secure the neckstrap before going back up through the same bugle bead, then through the entire neckstrap and down into the purse before finishing the thread securely amongst the seed beads.

This neck strap is quite simple but the use of a variety of different beads makes it particularly attractive.

Handy hint
Change rows and change threads on the back of the purse not the sides or front

Fringe

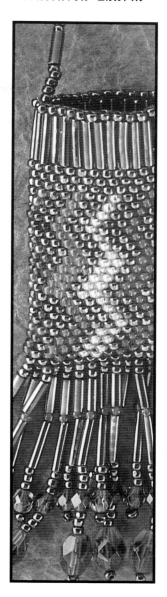

There is one row of fringe on this purse with strands of two different lengths. The shorter strand has the topaz coloured beads as a feature at the base of each strand and the longer row has an 8 mm smoky blue cut crystal bead as a feature at the base of each strand. The combination of these colours together in the fringe is most effective.

To make a fringe cut a 1.5 m length of thread and wax. Secure the thread firmly in the 'body' of the purse bringing the needle out at the bottom left hand corner of the purse, catch the thread securely in the oversewing across the base of the purse.
Always start each strand of the fringe with two seed beads.

The longer strand of the fringe has the two seed beads, (mentioned above) one 7 mm bugle bead, one bright blue bead, another 7 mm bugle, three main colour beads a 4 mm smoky blue crystal bead, three more main colour beads, then an 8 mm smoky blue crystal bead and is turned with a main colour seed bead. (For detailed information on turning beads please refer to page 8.) Take the needle back up the strand catch in the oversewing before starting the second strand.

The second strand of the fringe has the two seed beads, one 7 mm bugle bead one bright blue seed bead, another 7 mm bugle, three main colour seed beads a 4 mm topaz bead and is 'turned' on a main colour seed bead. Take the needle back up through all the beads on the strand of the fringe and catch it through the oversewing on the base of the purse. Work these two strands alternately across the base of the purse. On completion of the fringe finish your thread in the body of the purse in the usual way. Now wear your purse and enjoy it!

– Pink Parfait –

This amulet purse features a simple-to-follow pattern of five daisies and is made in circular brick stitch. It is made using seed beads for the body of the purse with a row of contrasting seed beads as a decorative feature at the top of the purse rather than bugle beads. The lush fringe features steel grey bugle beads along with the contrast beads used in the purse and special feature beads at the end of each tassel of the fringe.

Materials

- 10 grams size 11 rose pink (Mill Hill 00553*) seed beads (main colour)

- 5 grams size 11 amethyst beads for the three central daisies

- 2 grams size 11 pale pink matt beads for the two outer daisies

- 5 grams size 11 gold for the daisy centre also used in fringe and neckstrap

- 5 grams steel grey 12 mm bugle beads (medium or small could be used)

- 20 x size 6 mm round amethyst beads (fringe)

- 20 x 15 mm drops (fringe)

- 2 x 10 mm feature beads on the neckstrap (optional)

- Nymo® thread to match

- wax

- two short beading needles

*it is not recommended to wear these beads directly against your skin

refer to the colour photograph on page 37

Technique

circular brick stitch

Instructions

First row - foundation row

Cut a 1.5 m length of thread, wax and thread both ends with a beading needle then pick up one bead in your main colour, positioning it in the middle of your thread, (fig. 1).

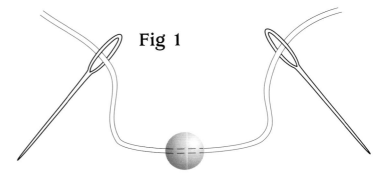

Fig 1

Fig 2

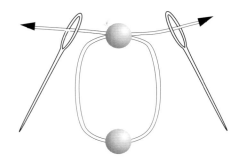

Fig 3

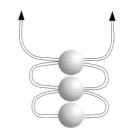

Pick up a second main colour bead and thread a needle through it from each end, (fig. 2). Repeat with a third bead fig. 3).

Fig 4

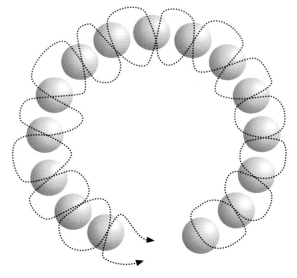

Continue in this manner until 42 beads have been threaded. Join in a circle by taking both threads back through the first bead, continue threading through two or three more beads to form a firm circle (fig. 4 & 4a). Take off one needle.

Fig 4a

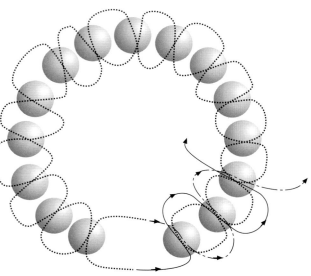

*Pick up two main colour beads and stitching towards yourself, bring the needle under the thread between the second and third bead in the previous row (fig. 5). Now take the needle back up through the second bead (fig. 6).

Do not pull the first two beads too tight as the first bead must have sufficient thread to sit down flat when it is stitched in place at the end of the first row.

Now pick up *just one* main colour bead and take the needle under the thread joining the third and fourth beads together, return the needle back up through the centre of the seed bead, continue in this way working around the circle picking up one bead at a time, taking the thread under the thread between the beads on the foundation row and back up the seed bead each time until the end of the row (fig. 7).

At the end of the row go down through the first bead, take the needle under the thread between the previous row of beads and come back up the first bead in the usual way.*

Second row

Work as for the first * - *.

Fig 5

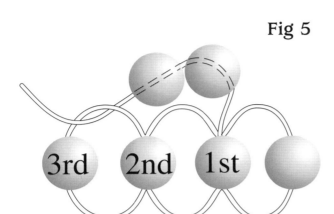

Fig 6

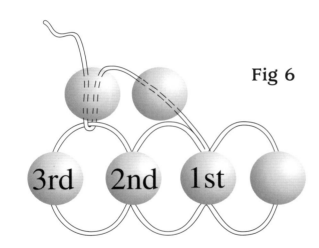

Fig 7

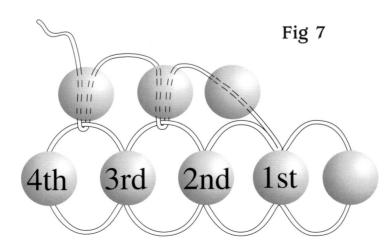

Handy Hint
Count 42 beads for each row and keep them separate to ensure that you stitch the right number of beads on each row of your purse.

'Pink Parfait'

'Clematis'

37

'Dawn'

'Lariat'

Rope necklace

'Fireworks'

39

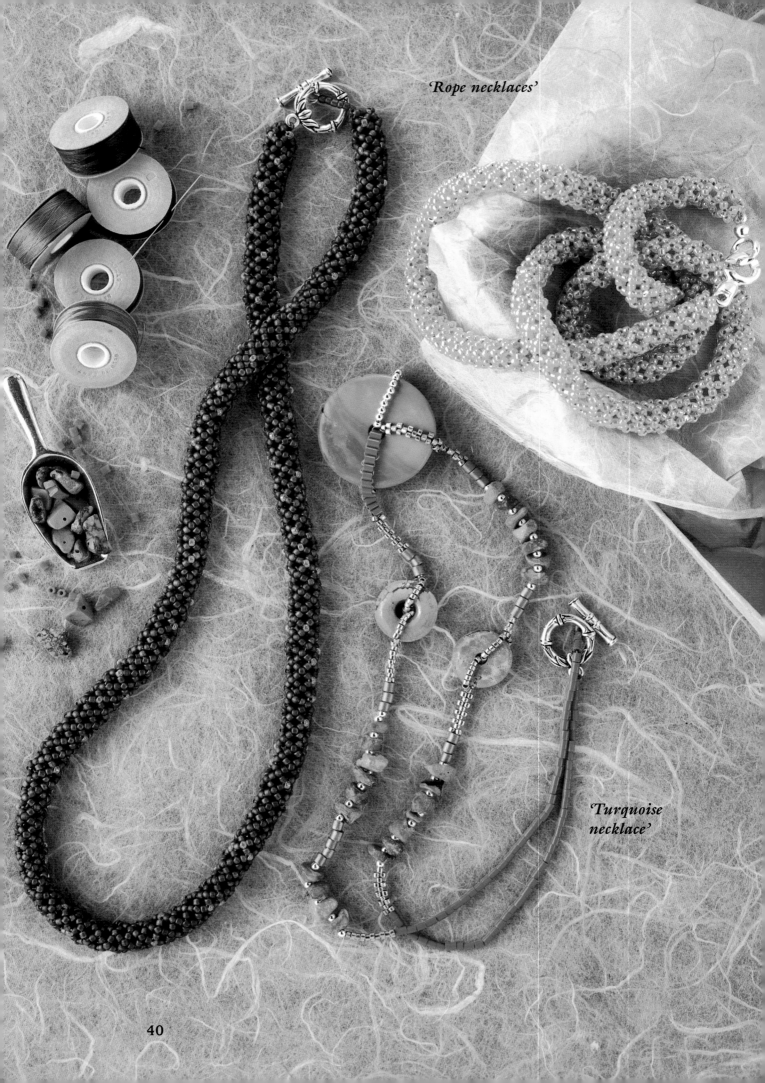

'Rope necklaces'

'Turquoise necklace'

40

'Fractured charm'

'Midnight on the beach'

41

'Evening Star'

'Black Sophisticate'

'Rope Necklace'

'Rope Bracelet'

'Exotic Bead Necklace'

'Sculptured Bracelet
and Necklace'

Following the Chart

When making an amulet purse in circular brick stitch you start at the top of the purse and work up from the foundation row. For this reason you start at the bottom of the chart and work up. The arrow shows the starting point.

Third Row

The pattern starts with the third row and is worked on the front of the purse only. To follow the chart and centre the design work 12 main colour beads continue by working two pale pink beads, two gold then two more pale pink beads, complete the row using the main colour beads.

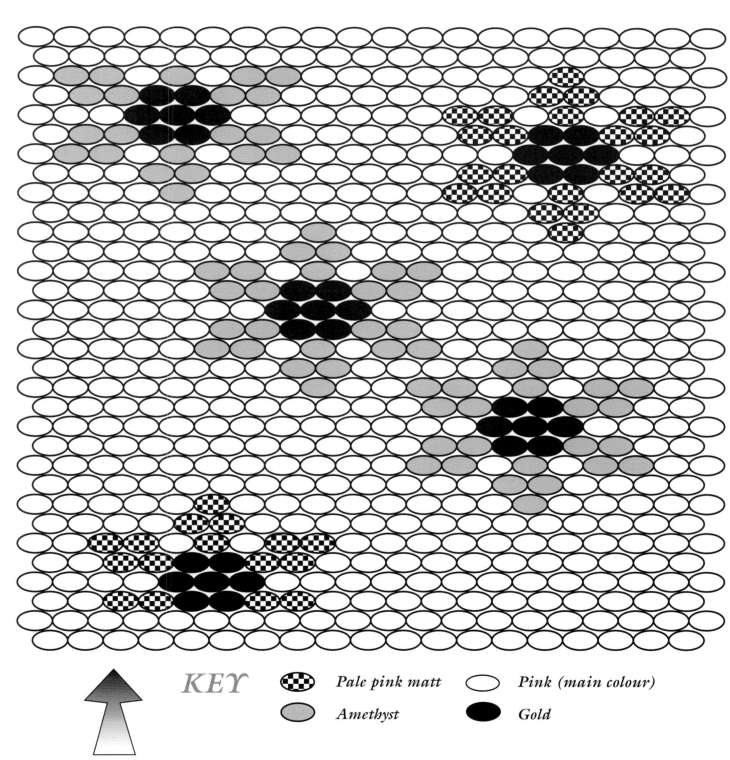

KEY

⬕ Pale pink matt   ⬭ Pink (main colour)

⬭ Amethyst   ⬬ Gold

As you are working put a line through the chart, or use felt tip pens to mark off the area you have worked. Making a pattern is very satisfying - you keep on wanting to do one more row to see the pattern grow!

Work five rows stitching to the right and then reverse your stitching and work five rows to the left. Change in this way throughout the purse to prevent a bias forming. If you run out of thread whilst stitching your purse refer to page 9 for detailed information on changing threads when working circular brick stitch.

When you have completed the pattern, centre the design and oversew across the bottom firmly. It is important to sew the purse firmly together at the base as the fringe is attached to this oversewing. Finish the thread end into the body of the purse. Refer to page 8 for detailed information on finishing.

Go back to the top of the purse and using the thread left at the very beginning, sew a row of contrast (amethyst) seed beads on top of the foundation row in the usual way (figs 5 & 6) to complete the purse. Finish the thread off securely. This can be done at any time during the construction of the purse.

Handy hint
Change rows and change threads on the back of the purse not the sides or front

Neck Strap

Cut a length of thread, twice the desired length plus 50 cm, wax. The thread is doubled to get the desired length but you actually work with a single thread. Attach the thread securely in the seed beads in the main body of the purse. Then take the thread up to the top of the purse at one side and pick up five main colour seed beads, one gold, one feature bead and then make a pleasing arrangement using the silver bugle beads, and the gold and pink seed beads until you reach the half way point. Now reverse your arrangement of beads until you are back to the final five seed beads, which match the beginning. See colour photograph page 37 for additional detail.

Take your thread down through five beads in the body of the purse, work the odd clove hitch amongst the seed beads to secure the neckstrap before going back up to the start of the neckstrap.

On the return trip pick up five main colour beads so that there are two lines of beads entering the gold seed bead and then the feature bead, from that point the needle goes through all the beads. To give added interest the pink beads between the two groups of grey bugle beads have been worked in peyote stitch. To work peyote stitch pick up a bead, miss a bead then take the needle through the next bead (fig. 8). Don't forget when you reach the feature and gold bead on the other side pick up five seed beads before taking the needle back down through five beads before finished off in the usual manner.

Fig 8

peyote stitch on neck strap

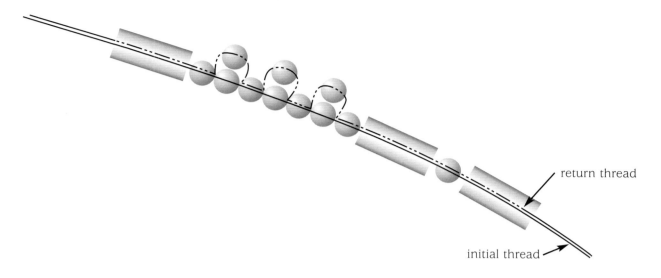

return thread

initial thread

Fringe

The fringe on this amulet purse is rather luxuriant! It has two rows, a shorter one at the front featuring a 6 mm amethyst bead and a longer one at the back with each strand finished with a pale amethyst drop.

To make a fringe cut a 1.5 m length of thread and wax. Secure the thread firmly in the 'body' of the purse bringing the needle out at the bottom left hand corner of the purse, catch the thread securely in the oversewing across the base of the purse.
Always start each strand of the fringe with two seed beads.

The first strand of the front row of the fringe has the two main seed beads, (mentioned above) one bugle bead, 12 amethyst seed beads, a 6 mm amethyst bead and is turned with an amethyst seed bead. For more detailed information on 'turning' refer to page 8. Take the needle back up through all the beads on the strand catch the thread into the oversewing across the bottom of the purse, move along one bead and start the next strand of the fringe. Each strand of the fringe is worked in the same way. On completion of the row of fringe, finish the thread in the body of the purse in the usual way.

Take a second 1.5 m length of thread, wax and bring it out once again at the bottom left hand side of the purse behind the front row of fringe. Catch it securely in the oversewing across the base of the purse.
The second row of the fringe has the two seed beads, one bugle bead and one amethyst bead (twice) a further bugle bead two gold beads and a is turned on the drop. Take the needle back up the strand anchor your thread in the oversewing at the base of the bag ready to continue with the next strand. All the strands in this row are worked in the same way. Finish the thread in the body of the purse in the usual way. Your purse is complete, enjoy it.

Black is a very popular colour for day and evening and this amulet purse is the perfect way to add that little 'extra' to a special outfit. The subtle design is made using three different toned gold beads. The simple fringe has strands of black seed beads alternating with long twisted bugle beads. Feature beads at the end of each strand complete the fringe. This design could be made up in many different colourways - it would look pretty in shades of one colour or very dramatic in primary colours!

Materials

- 10 grams size 11 black seed beads main colour
- 2 grams each of three different shades of gold size 11 seed beads
- 5 grams 7 mm black bugle beads (used at the top of the purse)
- 12 x 30 mm black twisted bugle beads (fringe)
- 12 x 1 cm black drops (fringe)
- 10 grams size 6 black beads (fringe and neck strap)
- 5 grams size 8 black beads (neckstrap)
- 8 x 8 mm cut jet beads (neck strap)
- black Nymo® thread
- wax
- two short beading needles

refer to the colour photograph on page 42

Technique

circular brick stitch

Instructions

Foundation row - bugle beads
The top of the purse is made using the 7 mm black bugle beads. Cut a 1.5 m length of thread, wax and thread both ends with a beading needle then pick up one black bugle

bead positioning it in the middle of your thread (fig 1). Pick up a second bugle bead and thread a needle

Fig 1

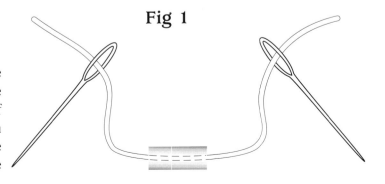

Fig 2

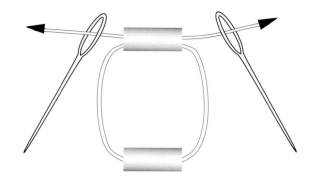

through it from each end (fig 2). Position the second bead on top of the first bead, repeat with a third bead (fig. 3). It is important that the bugle beads are not pulled too tightly together when you are stitching them as the seed beads which are worked in the next row are a little bigger than the bugle beads and won't sit nicely if the bugle beads are stitched too tightly.

Fig 3

Fig 4

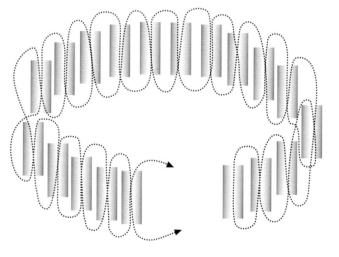

Continue in this manner until 42 bugle beads have been threaded. Join in a circle by taking both threads back through the first bead, continue threading through two or three more beads to form a firm circle and finish with one needle on each side of the beads (fig. 4 & 4a). Take off one needle.

Fig 4a

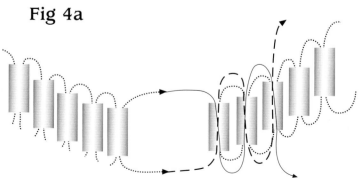

Rows 1 & 2 - seed beads

*Using your main colour (black) seed beads pick up two seed beads and stitching towards yourself, bring the needle under the thread between the second and third bugle bead (fig. 5).

Now take the needle back up through the second bead (fig. 6).
Do not pull the first two beads too tight as the first bead must have sufficient thread to sit down flat when it is stitched in place at the end of the first row.

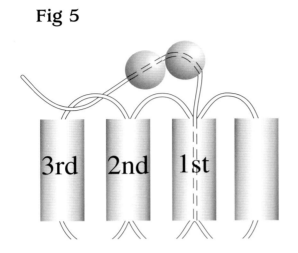

Fig 5

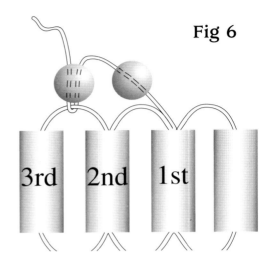

Fig 6

Now pick up *just one* seed bead and take the needle under the thread joining the third and fourth bugle beads together. Return the needle back up through the centre of the seed bead. Continue in this way working around the circle picking up one bead at a time, taking the needle under the thread between the beads in the previous row and back up the seed bead each time until the end of the row (fig. 7).

At the end of the row go down through the first bead, take the needle under the thread between the beads and come back up the first bead in the usual way.*

The first two rows in the purse are worked in the main colour only from * - *.

Starting second and all subsequent rows of seed beads (fig. 8).

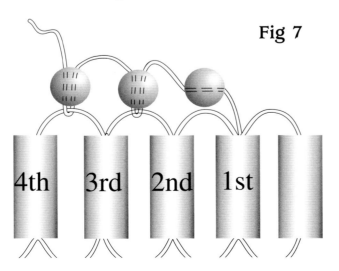

Fig 7

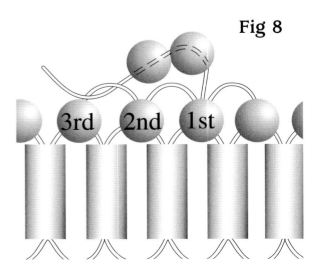

Fig 8

Following the Chart

When making an amulet purse in circular brick stitch you start at the top of the purse with the row of bugle beads and work up from these. For this reason you start at the bottom of the chart and work up. The arrow shows the starting point.

Row 3 - start of pattern to finish

The pattern starts in the third row and it is only worked on the front of the purse. Decide where each of the gold beads is to be used and mark on the bead boxes or in your bead dish the symbols which relate to each bead. To follow the chart and centre the design, work twenty main beads then

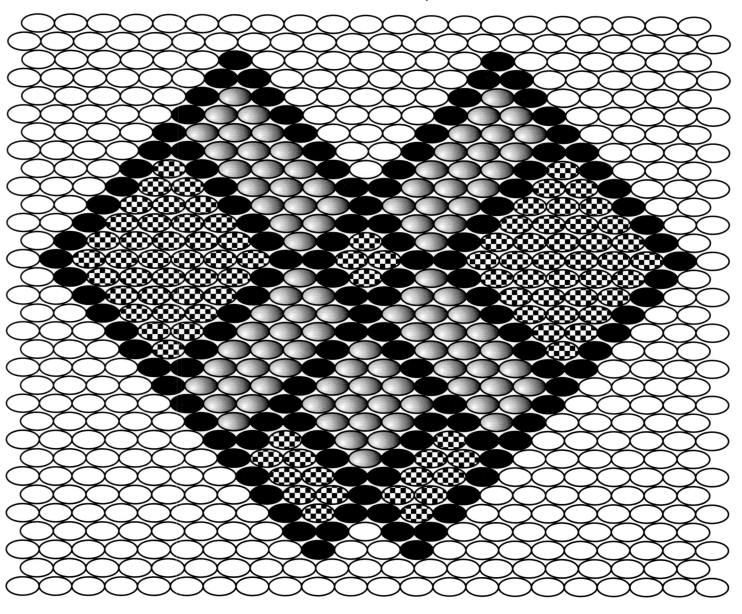

KEY

⬭   *Black (main colour)*

▦   *Gold shade 1*

⬭   *Gold shade 2*

⬬   *Gold shade 3*

51

follow the chart by stitching with the appropriate beads - one outline bead two main colour beads, one outline and then main colour beads for the rest of the row. As you are working put a line through the chart, or use felt tip pens to mark off the area you have worked. Complete your purse by following the chart and working in the usual way.

Work five rows stitching to the right and then reverse your stitching and work five rows to the left. Change in this way throughout the purse to prevent a bias forming.
If you run out of thread whilst stitching your purse refer to page 9 for detailed information on changing threads when working circular brick stitch.

When you have completed the purse centre the design and oversew across the bottom firmly. It is important to sew the purse firmly together at the base as the fringe is attached to this oversewing. Finish the thread end into the body of the purse. Refer to page 8 for detailed information on finishing.

Go back to the top of the purse and using the thread left at the very beginning sew a row of seed beads on top of the bugle beads in the usual way to complete the purse. Finish the thread off securely. This can be done at any time during the construction of the purse.

Handy hint
When using bugles, try using twisted bugles as they catch the light well

Neck Strap

The neck strap in this necklace is quite simple but particularly attractive in the arrangement of the different beads that have been used in it. Whilst we give the pattern, it is given as a guide only, do not follow it if you don't want to - take your beads and make an arrangement that pleases you - this is part of the fun.

Cut a length of thread, twice the desired length plus 50 cm, wax. The thread is doubled to get the desired length but you actually work with a single thread. Attach the thread securely in the seed beads below the bugle beads in the main body of the purse. Then take the thread up through the bugle beads to one side, at the top of the purse. Pick up five seed beads and one jet bead four times then five more seed beads. I then alternated two size 8 beads with one size 6 bead until the half way point.

The arrangement is then reversed until you are back to the final five seed beads, which match the beginning. Take your thread down through the bugle beads and work through some of the seed beads, working the odd clove hitch to secure the neckstrap before going back up through the same bugle bead, then through the entire neckstrap and down into the purse before finishing the thread securely amongst the seed beads.

On the return trip I picked up five beads so that there are two lines of beads entering the first jet bead, from that point the needle goes through all the beads until the last jet bead where five seed beads are picked up before the needle is taken back down through the bugle beads to be finished off in the usual manner.

Fringe

To make a fringe cut a 1.5 m length of thread and wax. Secure the thread firmly in the 'body' of the purse bringing the needle out at the bottom left hand corner of the purse, catch the thread securely in the oversewing across the base of the purse.

Always start each strand of the fringe with two seed beads. You may find it easier to make this fringe if you use a long beading needle.

The first strand of the fringe has the two seed beads, (mentioned above) one long twisted bugle bead, four seed beads, a size 6 bead, then a seed bead turning on a drop, then return the needle back up through all the beads on the strand and anchor it securely into the oversewing at the bottom of the bag. Move along one bead to start the next strand.

This strand has 26 seed beads then a size 6 bead with a further seed bead as a 'turning' bead. (For more information on turning beads refer to page 8.) Take the needle back up through the beads in this strand before anchoring the thread. Continue to work the remaining strands of the fringe, alternating the two different bead patterns. This purse will have 21 strands to the fringe. When you have completed it - just enjoy it!

Handy Hint
Count out 42 seed beads for each row to ensure that you stitch the right number of beads on each row of your purse.

Rope Bracelet and Necklace

The Rope Necklaces and Bracelet have been stitched in a honeycomb technique. This technique is easy to do and produces an attractive tubular effect. Interesting colour shading can be achieved by varying the colours used or you can use just one colour for your necklace or bracelet with the contrast bead being an antique bead for example rather than frosted. The contrast bead makes following this pattern very simple so for the first project using this technique I would advise using a contrast bead, though you may choose not to for later projects.

Materials

Bracelet

- 10 grams size 11 seed beads I used a variety of blue and purple toned beads
- 2 grams size 11 seed beads (contrast) I used silver beads
- Nymo® thread to match
- wax
- short beading needle
- clasp

Necklace

(quantities given for the pale aqua necklace page 40)

- 25 grams size 11 seed beads I used jade opaque beads
- 3 grams size 11 seed beads (contrast) I used jade lustre beads
- clasp

Refer to the colour photographs on pages 40 & 43

Technique

Honeycomb stitch

Instructions

Cut and wax a 1.5 m length of thread. Run the thread through the wax a couple of times before you begin and then throughout the time you are beading, wax the thread frequently.

First Circle

Pick up six beads in the main colour, go back through the first bead (A) to make a circle. Leave a 30 cm length of thread at the beginning for attaching the clasp (fig. 1).

Fig 1

30cm length of thread

Fig 2

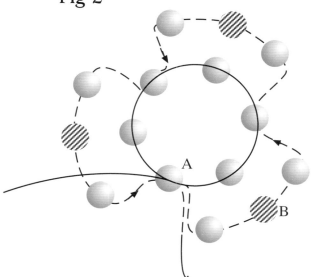

Second Circle (dashed line)

Keep the 30 cm length of thread firmly wrapped around the fingers of your left hand.

Pick up three beads (one main colour, one contrast and one main colour), miss a bead and go through the next. Repeat twice. Keep the beads firmly between the thumb and first finger of your left hand so that you do not change directions by mistake (fig. 2).

Fig 3

Third Circle

Continue picking up three beads (one main colour, one contrast and one main colour), but in this circlet you go through the contrast bead each time. You will go through the contrast bead (B) next but one from where your thread is for the first stitch but for the next three stitches there are three main coloured beads between the contrast beads (fig. 3)

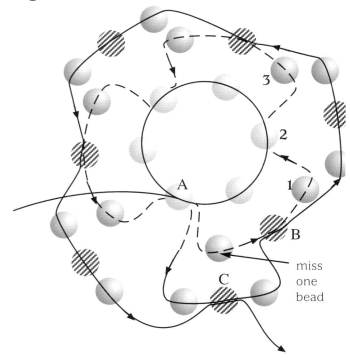

miss one bead

Fourth and continuing circles (fourth circle - dotted line)

Before continuing any further pull the 30 cm length firmly from the left and the thread in the needle firmly from the right and the beads will, with a little encouragement, form a little 'vessel' in appearance with the beads coming forward to form a hollow tube which is closed at the base - this is where the clasp will be attached later. You now work on the beads in this tube shape for the rest of your stitching. Keep a little tension on the thread to ensure the right 'tubular' shape develops.

As before pick up three beads (one main colour, one contrast and one main colour), miss three beads and go through the next contrast bead. You will notice that the missed three beads include one main, one contrast and one main bead, the contrast bead may not be noticed as it is pulled below the main bead on either side of it (fig. 4).

Keep working until you have reached the correct length for a necklace - 58 cm, bracelet - 21 cm, adjust as desired, - remember to allow for the width of the clasp in the bracelet.

Fig 4

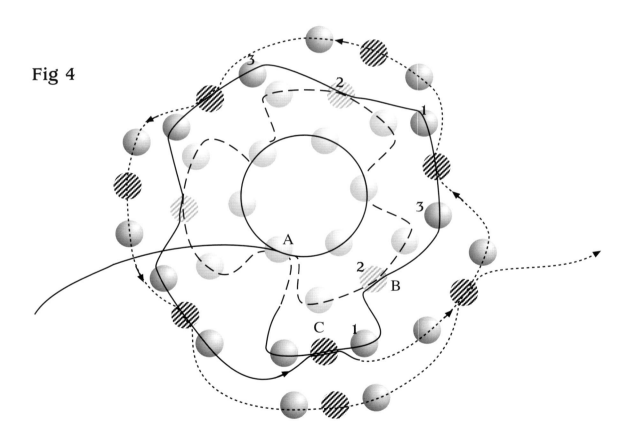

Handy Hint
Remember to run your thread through the wax frequently when beading.

Running out of thread in the middle of your necklace/bracelet

Bring in a new thread when you have about 20 - 30 cm of thread left. Take a further 1.5 m of thread, wax well and then bring it through to where the 'old' thread is and continue working, this way you will keep the pattern correct. When you have worked a few more rows go back and finish the two trailing ends in the usual manner.

Finishing

To finish, take your needle through the three last contrast beads to draw in the 'tube' before attaching the clasp. If you are using a hoop and bar clasp (as shown in the photograph) join six seed beads on the bar end before attaching the bar - to enable the bar to be easily manoeuvred through the hoop. Attach clasp firmly.

Finish the thread ends by working over a distance of at least 3 cm doing one catch stitch then threading the needle through a small number of beads, repeat this at least three times. This is a loose weave so extra care must be taken when finishing off the thread ends.

This is a most enjoyable beading technique. You will find you soon establish a rhythm and it is most satisfying to see the necklace growing. There are lots of possibilities, we have made it in red, gold and two shades of aqua, you could make it in a colour to suit a particular outfit or make one, shading it through a range of colours to go with many outfits!

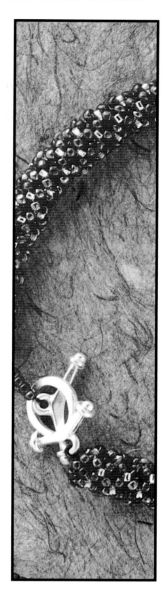

**Handy Hint
Interesting tonal variations have been achieved in the bracelet by using for examples two or three different shades of blue and purple beads along with the contrast silver bead.**

A red fringed vessel

Beads are a lot of fun to work with. Beaded necklaces and amulet purses have introduced you to the pleasure of working with beads. Try something a little different with the red fringed beaded vessel featured on page 39 or the hand painted vessel on page 38. The red fringed vessel has a swirling pattern in shades of red on the side of the vessel with a heavily fringed top. Making a design on a vessel is easy and enjoyable, see our instructions below. The little hand painted vessel with matching lid, has been made with clear glass beads and then painted on its completion. Both these vessels are enjoyable and satisfying to make and look most attractive on completion.

Materials

- 30 grams of size 11 beads (I used 5 grams each of six different shades of red, one 'main' colour for the background, five shades for the pattern)

- 10 grams of size 11 beads of your main colour for the fringe

- short beading needle

- wax

- Nymo® thread

- 7 cm diameter polystyrene ball

- glass headed pins

Refer to the colour photograph on page 39

Technique

circular brick stitch, increasing and decreasing

Fig 1

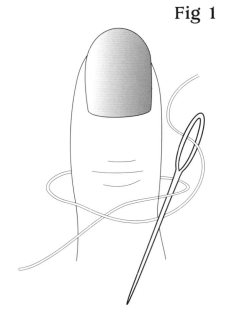

Instructions

Cut a 1.5 m length of thread, wax and thread with a short beading needle. Wrap the thread round your thumb once leaving a 10 cm tail of thread and work two buttonhole stitches into the thread, (fig. 1 & 2). You have now formed a circle of thread with a short tail of thread coming from the two buttonhole stitches at one side and a long thread with needle coming from the other side. Check that the short 'tail' of thread pulls the circle smaller (it is important that the short tail tightens the circle) (fig. 3). Slip the loop over the forefinger of your left hand. Tighten the loop and put your thumb over the knot to hold it firm.

Fig 2

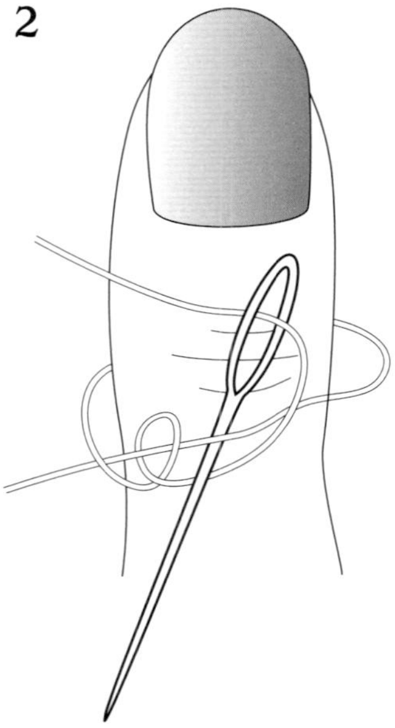

Fig 3

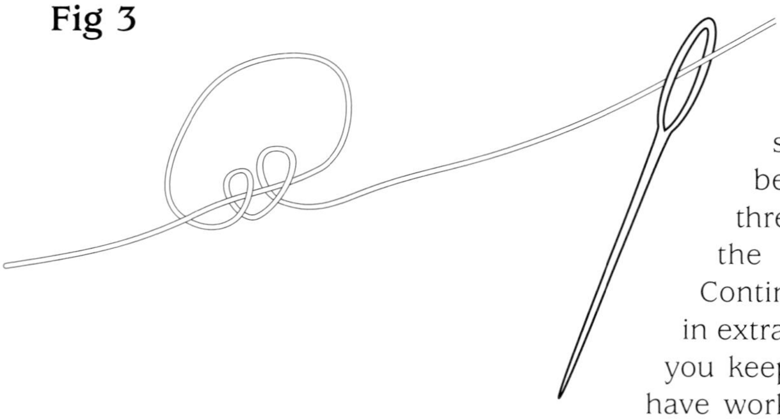

Fig 4

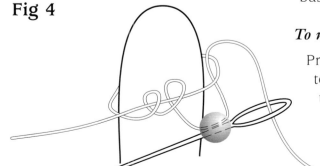

To Make the Base

*use main colour beads

Pick up one bead. Take the needle under the looped thread and then take the needle back through the bead (fig. 4). Pull the thread firmly and position the bead close to the two slip stitches. Add two more beads to the loop in the same way. Then carefully pull the short 'tail' to close the circle up tightly (fig. 5).

Holding the little circlet of beads firmly between your thumb and forefinger pick up a bead and attach it to the thread on the outside of the first bead in the same way as before. (Pick up one bead at a time, take the needle under the looped thread before taking the needle back through the bead.) Continue in this manner, working round and round the circle of beads. When working the first row out from the centre three beads, it can be difficult to find the thread between the beads to stitch into but after the first row it is easy.

If the beads do not sit snugly together stitch two beads into the same loop of thread between the beads in the previous row (fig. 6). Continue spiralling out, adding in extra beads as required so that you keep the work flat, until you have worked a 2.5 cm circle. Your base is complete.

To make the vessel side

Press the polystyrene ball firmly on to a hard surface to flatten a little, this will be the base of your vessel. If you want to work a design on your vessel draw the design on the polystyrene ball with a fine felt tip pen.

Fig 5

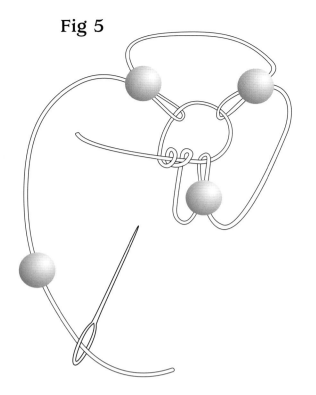

Fig 6

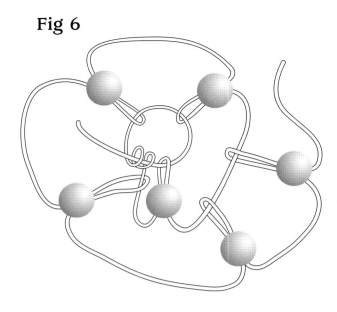

Colour in as a guide. Draw the finishing line - at least three quarters of the way up the ball. You will not follow the pattern lines exactly so it is better to have curved lines rather than straight ones.

Position the bead base on the flattened base of the polystyrene ball and pin in place. Use about five glass headed pins (as they are easier to remove) and move the pins up the work as you go to keep it firm.

To start the spiral pattern work five beads in the first pattern colour then five of the second etc continuing until all five pattern colours have been used then add five main colour beads. (The number of beads used could vary depending on the size of the base.) Repeat this until you are back to the start. In each succeeding row move on two beads for the colour change or change at the pen lines.

Fig 7

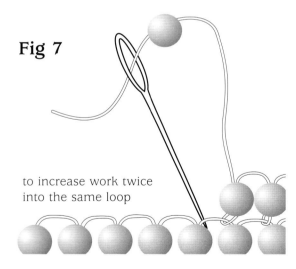

to increase work twice into the same loop

Fig 8

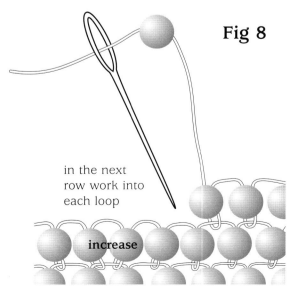

in the next row work into each loop

increase

Continue working in the same way - pick up one bead at a time, take the needle under the thread before taking the needle back through the bead - increase as required as the diameter of the polystyrene ball increases (figs 7 & 8). Do not increase too much (add too many extra beads) as this will form creases in your work. It is better to have tiny holes in your vessel as these will not be noticed. Stitch firmly. Work up the ball, your stitching goes behind the thread and down then back through the bead.

If you run out of thread whilst stitching your vessel refer to page 9 for detailed information on changing threads when working circular brick stitch. You may remove the work from the ball to add a new thread until you reach half way.

When you get beyond the half way point you will need to start decreasing as you work round the ball. To do this miss the loop between two beads on one row (figs 9 & 10). Keep the work very close to the ball to ensure a nice shape.

Fig 9

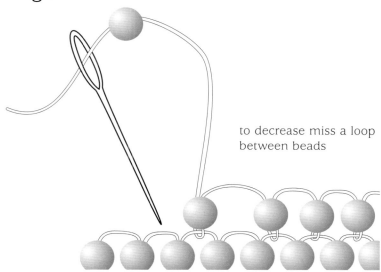

to decrease miss a loop between beads

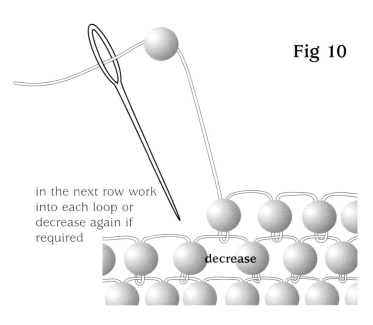

Fig 10

in the next row work into each loop or decrease again if required

decrease

When you reach the line drawn on the ball or the desired depth it is a rather nice finishing touch to work a single, final row of deeper coloured beads. You may notice that when you complete the last row the last bead of the row and the first are not exactly in line, this is unavoidable and will be hidden by the fringe.

Finish the thread off firmly, crush the ball and remove (I used an old vegetable knife to cut it). Now you can embellish the top!

Seaweed fringe

Cut a 1.5 m length of thread and wax. Start the thread in the usual way bringing it to just below the top. Catch the thread round the stitching between the top and second row of beads and pick up 18 size 11 beads, turning on the 18th bead (refer to page 8 for detailed notes on turning)

Take your needle back up two beads, this will give you three beads at the bottom, pick up three beads, to create a little 'branch'. Turn on the third bead and go back through the first two beads of the 'branch'. Now go up three beads of the main string and create another branch, do this until you reach the top (fig. 11).

At the top catch your thread between the top and second row of beads then take your thread down between every bead to make a luscious fringe.

My fringe is all the same length but if you preferred you could make it with strands of varying lengths and use a selection of different coloured beads.

Fig 11

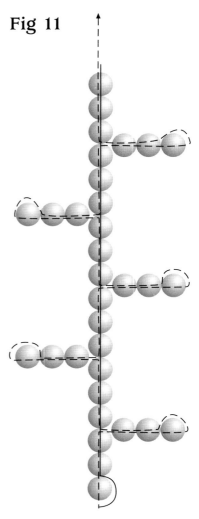

pick up 18 seed beads,
turning on the 18th.

A hand painted vessel with lid

This dainty little vessel evolved as I was making it. Initially I made it as I wanted to try painting on beads, then I thought it needs a lid' so it grew a little 'like Topsy'. Glass paints are freely available from Art Supply shops.

Materials

- 25 grams of clear glass size 11 beads

- Glass Dyes (available from art supply shops.)

- short beading needle

- wax

- Nymo® thread

- 2 x 5 cm diameter polystyrene balls

- glass headed pins

Refer to the colour photograph page 38

Technique

circular brick stitch, increasing and decreasing, making a lid

Instructions

Mark where the side of the vessel is going to be stitched up to on both balls before you start to ensure that the vessel and lid match nicely.

The base and sides of this vessel are made in the same way as the base and sides of the fringed beaded vessel. The only difference being that the base of this vessel is smaller, - 2 cm in diameter. (Refer to page 59)

To make a lid

You will need to use a new ball when making the lid, but do not flatten the base this time. Start as you did for the base of the vessel and when you have worked 1 cm pin the beads to the ball and continue working round, increasing as required until you have stitched down to the marked line.

Now remove the lid from the ball and continue working holding the lid in your hand. Gently spread the lid by increasing as required so that the lid will fit over the base. Work a further 6 rows before finishing off the thread in the usual manner.

With the vessel and lid complete they are ready for painting. Glass paints are delightfully easy to use. Just buy a few colours and then mix to create further colours. The painting is a lot of fun but over far too quickly!

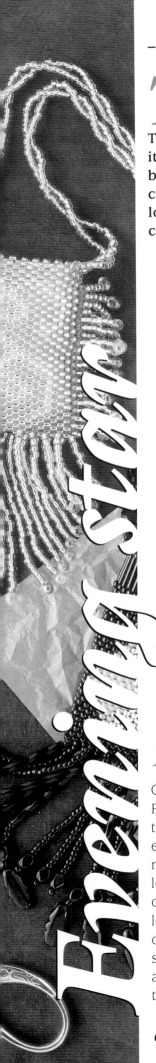

– Evening Star –

This Amulet Purse is the perfect accessory to add a sparkle to your evening! It has a simple geometric design in silver which adds subtle interest in tone to the otherwise golden appearance of the purse. The three sided fringe gives variety to your purse designs and whilst simple, it incorporates silver seed beads and small champagne coloured drop beads. The twisted neck strap is a worthy finale to complete a very elegant creation. This purse has been made using gold and silver beads it would look very dramatic black with a white contrast, for a softer appearance you could use two shades of the same colour. The possibilities are limitless!

Materials

- 30 grams size 11 transparent gold seed beads main colour

- 3 grams size 11 transparent silver seed beads (contrast)

- 4 grams 4 mm champagne coloured drops

- Nymo® thread

- wax

- short beading needle

- round cardboard tube (toilet roll centre!)

Refer to the colour photograph on page 42

Technique

even count Peyote Stitch

Instructions

Cut and wax a 1.5 m length of thread. Pick up 50 beads (main colour). Tie the beads in a circle 50 cm from the end of the length of thread, (fig. 1). Do not pull the beads tightly together - leave space for a further 2 - 3 beads on the thread. Cut your tube lengthwise, slide the circle of 50 beads on to the tube squashing the tube in so that the beads rest on it firmly but are not stretched tightly. Tape the tube to the correct size.

NOTE

This circle of 50 beads becomes rows 1 & 2 when you add the third row of beads. The pattern starts on row 4.

Row 3

To start the third row, working from right to left, take the needle back through the first bead to the left of the knot (bead A). The short tail of thread is now on the right of this bead.

Pick up a bead, miss a bead and go through bead number three (fig. 2). Pull the thread up tight so that the bead you are adding pushes the bead beneath it half way down the neighbouring beads (fig. 3).

Fig 1

Fig 2

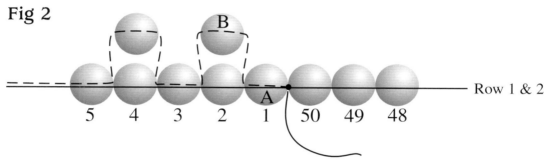

Fig 3

work in the same way.
You are now ready to begin row 4, the first row of the pattern.

I personally prefer to work up the tube if you prefer you may work down the tube, the end result is the same. Just work the way that feels more comfortable for you.

Continue to pick up a bead, miss a bead then take your needle through the next bead right round until you reach the end of the row.

After picking up the last bead of row three (bead Z) you must take the needle through the first bead of row three (bead A) and then take your needle through bead B (the first bead you picked up in this row) (fig. 4). By taking your bead through beads A and B you have made a 'step up' to the next row. At each row change you will be moving diagonally up across the

Handy Hint
Practice this technique using a smaller number of bigger beads for each row and working the different rows using different coloured beads. You will then see how it 'works'.

Fig 4

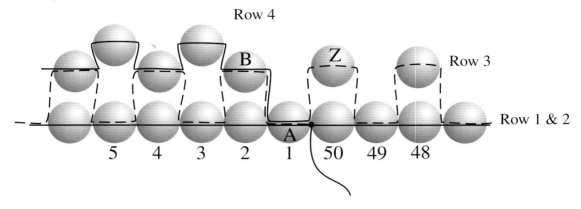

Row 4

B   Z   Row 3

Row 1 & 2

5   4   3   2   1   A   50   49   48

Row 4

Work 10 main colour beads before you begin your pattern with two contrast beads, two main colour, one contrast then main colour until the end of the row. Draw a line through each row of the pattern as you complete it so you don't lose your place.

Continue working following the pattern - just follow the pattern ignore the plain beads!

Always remembering that after picking up the last bead of the row you must take the needle through the first bead of the row and then through the first bead you picked up in this row, then pick up a new bead and continue the new row. (Refer to fig. 4 for the steps involved.)

When you have completed the pattern work two more rows using the main colour only. Centre the design and oversew across the bottom of the purse firmly. Finish off the thread, for detailed information on starting and finishing threads refer to page 8.

Neck strap

Cut two pieces of thread the desired length, plus 50 cm and wax. Join each thread to the top of one side of the bag in the usual manner having both threads coming out of the same bead so that the two strands of the neckstrap will twist together nicely. Thread each strand with main colour beads to the correct length for your neck strap. Hold both loose ends firmly together and wind the purse to twist the neckstrap. Sew ends firmly back into purse and finish in the usual manner.

Fringe

Cut a 1.5 m length of thread, wax and secure in the body of your purse bringing the thread out ready to begin the fringe between the third and fourth row down from the top at one edge. Pick up three main colour, one contrast, two main colour and one drop, turning on the drop return back to the purse and continue working down the purse putting a fringe made with the same combination of beads between each row. Across the base of the bag add two extra main colour beads to each strand of the fringe until you reach the centre then reduce each strand by two beads until you are back to the other side. Work the other side of the bag to match the first and then finish off thread securely.

Following the Chart

Once again you are working from the top of your purse down. This means that you work from the bottom of the chart up. The arrow shows the starting point.

Although you originally picked up 50 beads, these 50 beads became rows 1 & 2 and each row is actually only 25 beads long. On the chart row 4 beads are marked with a dot.

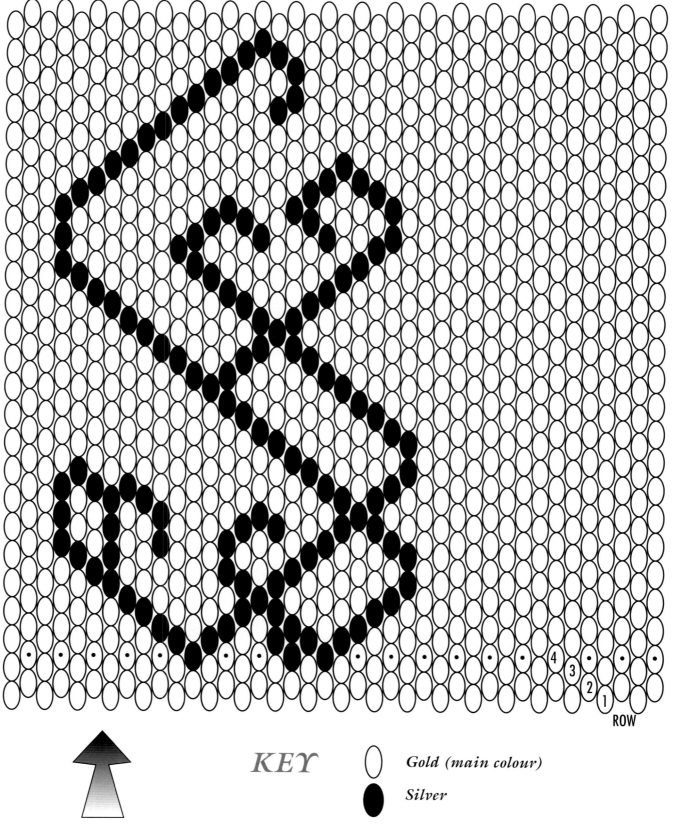

ROW

KEY

◯ *Gold (main colour)*

⬤ *Silver*

67

– Clematis –

Delica beads are very small tubular beads. For their size they have comparatively large holes making them ideal beads to use if many threads are going through each bead. They also lie very flat. Although these beads are described as size 11 they are really more like a size 14 making it possible to create a more delicate pattern than is possible with larger beads.

This bag has a shimmering elegance. A simple design of clematis flowers is worked amongst emerald, royal blue and purple beads to create a bag that you just can't resist touching, and stroking! All beads are very tactile, but delica beads are even more so. The luxuriant fringe in emerald and royal blue is a fascinating finale to a beautiful purse.

Materials

- 15 grams purple delica beads No. 135 (main colour)

- 15 grams emerald delica beads No. 27

- 5 grams royal blue delica beads No. 63

- 2 grams cream delica beads No. 203

- 1 gram yellow delica beads No. 53

- 50 size 6 (4 mm) jade beads, (fringe and neck strap)

- 4 size 6 (4 mm) amethyst beads (optional used on neckstrap only)

- Nymo® thread black

- wax

- two short beading needles

Refer to the colour photograph on page 37

Technique

Circular brick stitch purse, peyote stitch neckstrap.

Detailed information on starting and finishing threads is given on page 8.

Fig 1

Fig 2

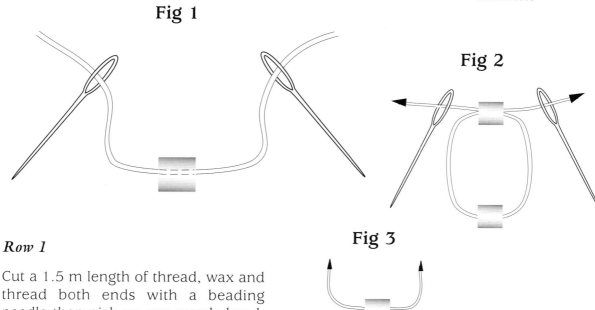

Row 1

Cut a 1.5 m length of thread, wax and thread both ends with a beading needle then pick up one purple bead, position it in the middle of your thread, (fig 1). Pick up a second purple bead and thread a needle through it from each end, (fig 2). Position the second, third and all subsequent beads on top of the first (fig. 3). Pick up a further 12 purple beads, 8 emerald and then 37 purple beads - 60 beads in total.

Fig 3

Join in a circle by taking both threads back through the first bead, continue threading through two or three more beads to form a firm circle and finish with one needle on each side of the beads (fig. 4 & 4a). Take off one needle.

Fig 4

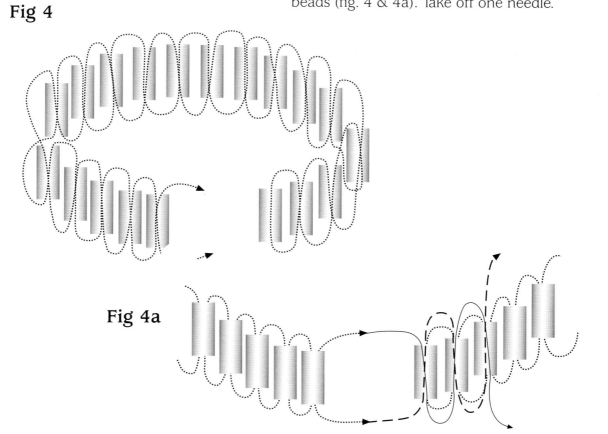

Fig 4a

Row 2 - finish

*Pick up two purple beads and stitching towards yourself, bring the needle under the thread between the second and third beads in the foundation row (fig. 5). Now take the needle back up through the second bead (fig. 6).

Do not pull the first two beads too tight as the first bead must have sufficient thread to sit down flat when it is stitched in place at the end of the first row.

Now pick up *just one* purple bead and take the needle under the thread joining the third and fourth beads together, return the needle back up through the centre of the bead (fig. 7). Continue in this way working around the circle, picking up one bead at a time and following the chart, until the end of the row.

At the end of the row go down through the first bead, take the needle under the thread in the previous row of beads and come back up the first bead in the usual way.*
Work all following rows as from * - * following the chart given on page 71 and stitching in the usual manner.

The pattern is only on the front of the bag.

Work five rows stitching to the right and then reverse your stitching and work five rows to the left. Change in this way throughout the purse to prevent a bias forming.

Fig 5

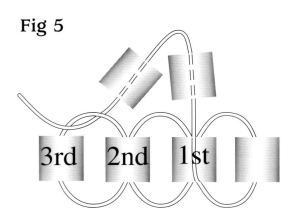

Fig 6

Fig 7

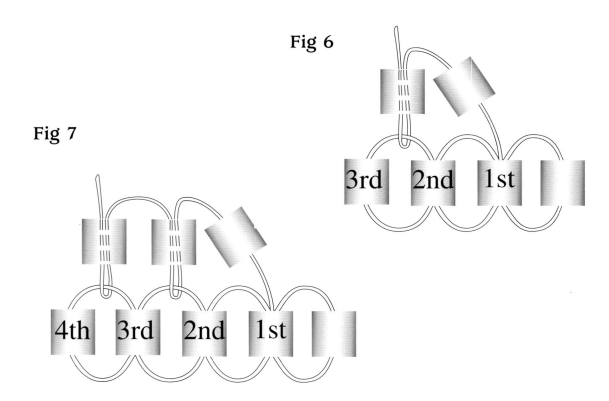

Following the chart

This purse is made in circular brick stitch. The first row is worked in delica beads (not bugles) and the pattern starts in the very first row. You start stitching at the top of the purse and work up. For this reason you start at the bottom of the chart and work up. The arrow shows the starting point.

Handy Hint
Put a pencil line through the pattern as you complete each line, or colour the area worked with felt tips.

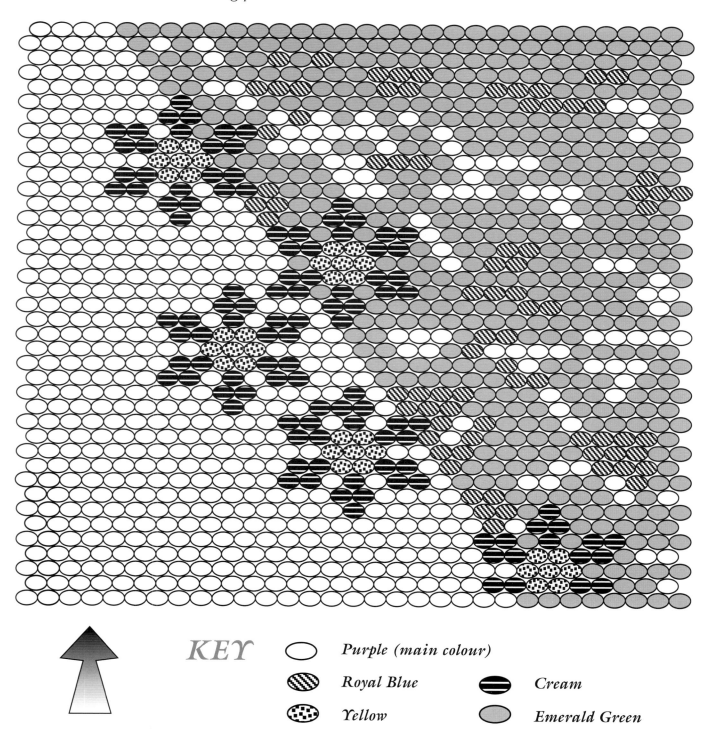

KEY

⬭ Purple (main colour)

▨ Royal Blue   ⬛ Cream

▩ Yellow   ⬭ Emerald Green

When you have completed the pattern, centre the design and oversew firmly across the bottom. It is important to sew the purse firmly together at the base as the fringe is attached to this oversewing. Finish off the thread in the body of the purse (for detailed information on finishing threads refer to page 8).

Go back to the top of the bag and finish off the beginning thread. Take a new thread 1.5 m in length and wax, take the thread to the top of the first row of beads and finish the top with a three bead scallop. To do this, bring your needle out at the top of your bag, pick up three purple delica beads and take your thread down through the next bead along, then back up the next bead and so on, (fig. 8). Continue in this way around the top of the bag, finish the thread in the body of the purse in the usual manner.

Fig 8

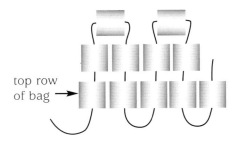

top row
of bag →

Seaweed fringe

Cut a 1.5m length of thread and wax. Secure the thread firmly in the body of the bag and then take your needle down to the left hand edge of the bag catching the thread securely round the oversewing at the base of the bag. Pick up 30 emerald beads, turning on the 30th bead. (For more detailed information on 'turning' refer to page 8.)

Take your needle back up two beads, this will give you three beads at the bottom, pick up three beads, to create a little 'branch'. Turn on the third bead and go back through the first two beads of the 'branch'. Now go up three beads of the main string and create another branch, do this until you reach the top (fig. 9). At the base of the bag catch the first strand into the oversewing before starting the second strand.

Fig 9

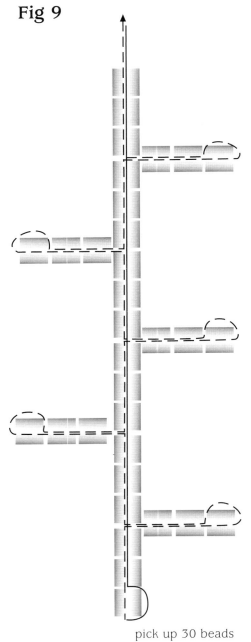

pick up 30 beads increasing to 60 as the fringe progresses

All the strands of the fringe are made with emerald beads except for five which are worked in royal blue, these are spaced across the base of the purse. Continue making the fringe as described and having a strand of the fringe between each bead on the bottom of the purse adding three additional beads to each strand until the string is 60 beads long, then reduce each strand by three beads until you reach the other edge of the bag. Add a 4 mm jade bead at random through the fringe. This is absolutely haphazard and gives the fringe that added interest.

Neck Strap

Cut a length of thread, twice the desired length plus 50 cm, wax. The thread is doubled to get the desired length but you actually work with a single thread. Attach the thread securely in the beads in the main body of the bag. Then take the thread up to the top of the bag at one side and pick up five purple beads, one 4 mm amethyst bead, (twice), five more

purple, then one 4 mm jade bead and 5 emerald beads (twice), one more 4 mm jade, 2 cm of emerald beads then 4 mm jade beads with 5 emerald beads in between (thrice). From this point I have used the emerald and purple delica beads randomly.

When you have reached the mid point of your neckstrap reverse your arrangement of beads until you are back to the final five purple beads, which match the beginning. Take your thread down to the body of the bag, working the odd clove hitch amongst the seed beads to secure the neckstrap before going back up through the entire neckstrap and back down into the body of the bag before finishing the thread securely amongst the seed beads. To give added interest to the neck strap I have worked all the delica beads in peyote stitch on the return trip. To work peyote stitch pick up a bead, miss a bead then take the needle through the next bead (fig. 10). Finish the end off firmly in the body of the bag. Now you can wear your beautiful purse and just wait for the compliments!

Fig 10

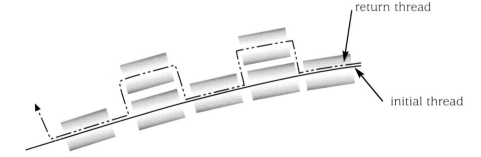

return thread

initial thread

Sculptured Bracelet

One of the joys of making a bracelet such as this is that it gives you a chance to use a variety of beads of different sizes and colours. Here is the perfect opportunity to use the odd quite large bead, unusual shaped beads, different coloured beads, try out new colour combinations, be creative and generally just enjoy 'fiddling' with beads!

Materials

- A variety of beads of different colours, shapes and sizes!

- Nymo® thread

- wax

- short beading needle

- clasp

Refer to the colour photograph on page 44

Technique

peyote stitch

Instructions

Cut a 1.5 m length of thread and wax. Tie a keeper bead 20 cm from one end of the thread (for detailed information on keeper beads please refer to page 8).

Pick up beads in groups of 10 - 15 at a time in various colours and sizes. Continue picking them up until you have enough beads to fit round your wrist - remember to allow for the clasp.

When you have picked up sufficient beads to go round your wrist, turn and and go back through the third to last bead, (this will form a nice 'square' edge) and work peyote stitch back to the beginning. To work peyote stitch pick up a bead, miss a bead and go into the next bead (fig. 1). Despite the interesting variations in this bracelet and its quite complex appearance it is worked entirely in peyote stitch!

Work back and forth along the length of the bracelet working 'clumps' of colour. Move the colour changes to prevent a straight line. Use smaller beads on one side of the bracelet and larger sized beads on the other and this will make the bracelet curve

Fig 1
to work a peyote stitch

turn and go back through third to last bead

nicely so that it sits most elegantly on your wrist.

You may like to leave a gap between the beads by making a bridge. To do this instead of working peyote stitch through - say nine beads just pick up nine beads then take your thread back into the nearest bead and continue working in peyote stitch. They are worked in peyote stitch in the next row (fig. 2).

To add a large bead just pick up the bead, position it and take your needle through it, you will miss a couple of beads (depending on how large your bead is) then take your thread back into the bead nearest the end of the large bead, (fig. 3).

To add loops either on the side or the surface, complete your bracelet then for a side loop bring the needle out of an edge bead, pick up the beads for the loop, say four to six, then take the thread through the bead nearest the end of the loop. For a surface loop

bring the needle out in the desired position pick up some beads (I picked up 14) before taking your thread through the bead nearest where you wish to position the end of the loop, (fig 4).

You can form a little scallop by going back and forth in a small area (fig. 5).

Sew some interesting beads, big or square, or specially coloured to the outside edges!

When you have completed your little masterpiece, remove the keeper bead and sew the catches on very firmly at both ends - bracelets do get quite a bit of wear! Now that you can see how easy this is to make, create a matching necklace and really create a stir!

Fig 4

to add a loop

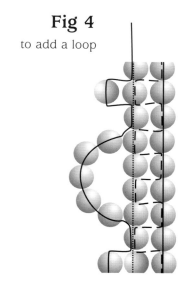

Fig 3

to add a large bead

Fig 2

to create a bridge

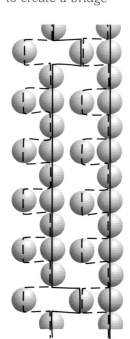

Fig 5 scallop

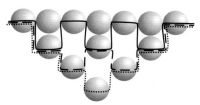

Sculptured Necklace

If you have already made the bracelet, you will have discovered the pleasure of working with beads to create a necklace like this. Once again you can use a great variety of beads of different sizes, shapes and colours! I have a feature stone as the focal point for this necklace (actual size 2.5 x 1.4 cm) plus a big assortment of beads in a range of sizes and colours. Choose the colours you like to wear and start - it is so much easier than it looks! The bracelet and necklace together create a very striking and different set of jewellery which would look equally attractive with denim or silk!

Materials

- A variety of beads of different colours, shapes and sizes!

- One large stone

- Nymo® thread

- wax

- short beading needle

- suede or leather to stick the stone to

- craft glue

- catch

Refer to the colour photograph on page 44

Technique

peyote stitch

Instructions

Before you can start stitching, glue the stone to the suede. Leave it to dry and then trim the suede back to just under the stone. Leave enough suede extending beyond the glue to stitch into.

Cut a 1.5 m length of thread and wax. Bring your needle up from the back of the leather to the right side with the stone facing you, leave a 20 cm tail and make a securing stitch.

Pick up a bead and take a stitch from the back to the front (stone facing you), take the needle down through the loop and pull firmly (fig. 1).

Continue to pick up a bead, take a stitch from back to front then take the needle down through the loop all the way round the stone. The beads should be just touching.
Make sure the beads stay on your left (if you are right handed) and sit up with the holes parallel to the edge of

the suede. When you have worked right round the suede run your needle and thread through all of the beads on the edge to make them line up perfectly.

Fig 1

Handy Hint
Check all beads
for rough edges
and discard

Work around this first row of beads in peyote stitch - to work peyote stitch pick up a bead, miss a bead go into the next bead, (fig. 2). Continue working in peyote stitch round the central stone for three rows, change the colours of the beads you are working with making sure that the colour changes are not in a straight line but rather work in 'clumps'. You will need to add in more beads when you are going round a curve. You can do this by adding in an extra bead or two or by adding a larger bead (fig 3). You may like to work extra rows on the lower edge of the stone.

The necklace is worked in sections or 'blocks' from this point on as it helps you to shape the necklace into a curve as you work. This is also done by stitching smaller beads on the inside curve and larger beads on the outside curve and ensures that the necklace fits the neck nicely.

Fig 2

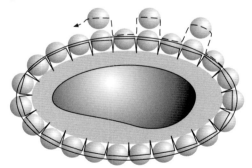

For clarity extra suede is shown - it should not be visible beyond the stone

Fig 3

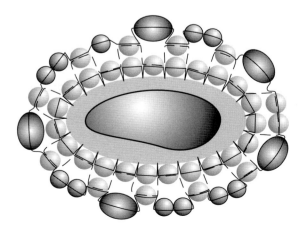

String 8 cms of beads, picking up 10 - 12 each of the various beads in different colours. Turn and go back through the third bead from the needle (fig. 3). This gives a nice turning edge and gives a square edge to work into on the next section. Peyote stitch back to the centre, catch into the main section and then return to the other end again. Peyote stitch back and forth for six to eight rows changing colour and style of bead. Finish off the thread and repeat on the other side.

Add extensions at each side approximately 8 cm at a time. Always join into the main (already stitched) piece each time you come to it. Work in this way until you reach the desired length. You can work peyote stitch on each side and this helps with shaping your necklace nicely.

When you feel your necklace is finished just look at it to check that it is harmonious in appearance - it is not supposed to be exact or equal - it is not that kind of necklace and if you feel there is a little gap you can always add a little more here or there! Beads may be added to the surface of the work by taking a string of 10 - 12 beads across the surface and anchoring, make a bridge on the edge - anything goes! (See sculptured bracelet for bridges, loops etc page 75). I actually added extra rows to the front of my necklace right at the end!

When your necklace is completed attach the clasp firmly and wear it with pride. It is unique!

Fig 4

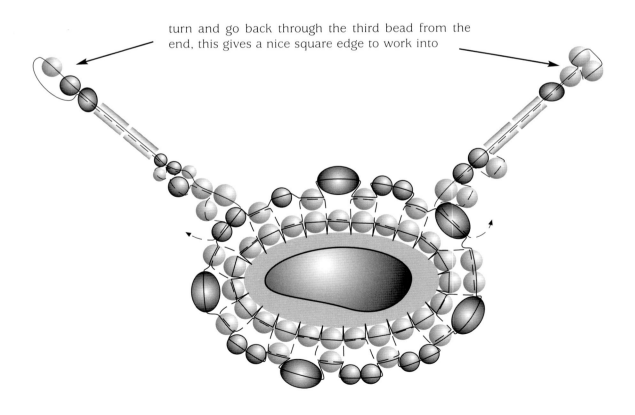

turn and go back through the third bead from the end, this gives a nice square edge to work into

Use chart this way for Circular Brick Stitch

Use chart this way for Peyote Stitch

Distributor
AUSTRALIAN DISTRIBUTOR

Stadia Trading Pty Limited

P.O. Box 357 Beaconsfield NSW Australia 2014
Tel: (612) 9565-4666 Fax: (612) 9565-4464
Email: stadia@stadia.com.au
Internet: http://www.stadia.com.au